The Bathroom Book

The Bathroom Book

THE ULTIMATE DESIGN RESOURCE FOR THE HOME'S MOST ESSENTIAL SPACE

EDITED BY BILL PARTSCH

Woman's Day® Specials   filipacchi publishing

Contents

Introduction

WHILE THEIR CORE PURPOSE REMAINS UNCHANGED, bathrooms today are a far cry from the utilitarian spaces of yesteryear. To a great extent, this is owed to advances in the fixtures and fittings that fill the room. For a rundown of these developments, read on.

Let's start with taking a shower. Sure, you can always opt for the traditional overhead spray—but more and more, designers and homeowners are looking to elevate the experience above the everyday by installing the latest in specialty fittings. A network of wall-mounted body jets, strategically placed throughout the shower enclosure, brings a fresh dimension to the daily drench. (DIYers, take note: shower panels are an easy retrofit alternative that deliver the essence of the body jet effect without having to break through the wall.) Hand showers, once considered a strictly European quirk, are now de rigueur in American households.

No longer confined to the health club, the steam shower has moved into the master suite. Models that incorporate aromatherapy convincingly replicate high-end spa treatments.

While jetted tubs have been on the scene for a while, improvements in "bubble technology" give today's bathers a choice of indulging in a relaxing or an invigorating soak. Air jets create a quiet rush of turbulence, while well-aimed water jets can massage specific muscle groups.

Toilets deliver not only efficient water consumption (they're mandated to have a 1.6-gallon flush), but now have posterior-pampering functions like automatic wash and dry features. Elevated seat heights and elongated bowls make commodes more comfortable for people of all ages and abilities.

Even bathroom storage has benefited from progress in product design. Borrowing a trick or two from cabinetry in the kitchen, vanities are now frequently fitted with pull-out mini-pantries that can hold towels and toiletries. Brushes and combs replace sponges and scrubbers in tilt-out sink panels, and appliance garages are home to hair driers and electric toothbrushes rather than blenders and coffeemakers.

These technological changes have often gone hand-in-glove with the aesthetic evolution of the room. As the culture of the bath continues to pursue a spalike direction, elements of Asian design are particularly visible. Natural materials, strong textures, neutral colors, and simple forms are hallmarks of this look.

Modernism also makes a stand in the bath with sleek lines and cubic compositions often rendered in tile and stone. Supplementing the standard ceramic tile, glass tile, ranging in size from mosaics to large formats, make the room shimmer in color and light.

The Bathroom Book will help you make the most of your master suite, family bath, or powder room by providing not only design inspiration for your dream space, but solid information on how to achieve it, too.

— LESLIE PLUMMER CLAGETT
Editor of Woman's Day Special Interest Publications *Kitchens & Baths*

Design Talk

What are the essential features of a bathroom?

A bathroom is a space where form meets function. Baths have functional requirements in places such as the lav, the shower and the toilet, where there should be a certain minimum number of inches of clearance. The toilet needs 36 inches; the lav needs at least 30 inches, if not more. The shower needs at least 32 inches, but here again, it should be at least 36. Going to 36 inches versus 32 for a lot of people is a lot of room—they feel they're lost, it's so spacious.

The design of the bathroom needs to incorporate form, too, and creating storage in such a small space can be a challenge. Using adjacent spaces such as closets or parts of adjacent bedrooms can help. If that's not an option, try using the 3½-inch space between the drywall studs.

Safety is also more of an issue in the bathroom than in the kitchen. Grab bars and non-skid surfaces are obviously important. Consider vision, too. Sight starts to deteriorate with age, so lighting is important. Surface contrast is important. A lighter color countertop to reflect light at the sink is preferable to a darker color. Try to get proper, even light at about 60 inches at the sink for shaving and makeup needs.

What should be the first fixtures selected when designing a bathroom?

From a design standpoint, the tub takes up the most room, but from a plumbing standpoint, the most difficult fixture to place is the toilet, because it has the largest drain size. The existing drain location and the direction of the joists will dictate the location of the toilet, because running a 3-inch drain pipe between two joists is much easier than trying to run it through joists. Shower and sink drains are two inches, which runs through joists more easily.

Again, for aesthetics, the tub will set the mood—because of its size—along with the faucets. Lav faucets set the tone and finishes for the whole room. As for the tub, a 66-inch version is the most comfortable, offering more room than the standard 60 inches without overwhelming. In a 72-

inch tub, shorter people's feet wouldn't reach the back wall. They'd just keep sliding down until they started floating. That's why some designers skip the tub in half of the baths they design: The shower is more of a priority. Huge spaces can include both, but when something gets sacrificed, it's the tub.

What is the most overrated feature in a bathroom design?

Whirlpools. A soaking tub is much more desirable in more people's minds. If a person really needs hydromassage, then a whirlpool tub can provide the oxygenation of the water to get into muscles. For the broad population, though, the appeal is less than definite. One designer found that 90% of the people in his staff he spoke to only used their whirlpool tubs two or three times a year. In most situations, a soaking tub is a much more desirable product. Most consumers would likely get more use out of a soaking tub, being able to relax in a deep tub without the noise and the motion. That said, a movement is afoot in the world of jetted tubs: Air tubs are becoming more popular. These differ from whirlpool tubs in that they circulate air rather than water. The motor of an air-jet tub can be mounted at a remote location in the home, thereby reducing the noise factor in the bathroom.

Another overrated design feature is anything with a step in it. Anything that requires a step up to get into will be very slippery getting out. Tiled and sunken tubs are way overrated, too. Tiled tubs are cold, they don't maintain the heat, they're very uncomfortable and they're hard to clean. Laying down in a sunken tub puts the bather at eye level with a Chihuahua, and unless that floor gets cleaned every hour on the hour, it gets messy with hair and dust—more than people would imagine.

What is the most underrated feature in a bathroom design?

That would be the shower, because the shower stall is the most important space for most people to get a daily experience. Don't skimp on the shower because of budget considerations; take the money from another portion of the budget. Showers are in a transformation process. A shower isn't just a shower anymore—it's a human car wash, with 10 or 20 luxurious showerheads. If you don't put in the body sprays and you don't put in the hand spray or the ceiling fixture, you may regret it later.

Should a bathroom design coordinate or contrast with a home's décor?

This issue prompts two schools of thought. One is that a home's décor should be consistent throughout. Subscribers to this school would say, "Absolutely, coordinate." In this way of thinking, making a personal statement in the home is best left to another room. It's best to think of the procession from hallway to bedroom to bathroom, with each step of the way leading into a more private space. This is not the path in which to introduce some radical new design.

PRECEDING PAGES: Bathrooms have become retreats, with bathing fixtures that rejuvenate and places to relax.

ABOVE: Whirlpool tubs are great for those who truly need hydromassage. Those who don't might get more pleasure from a deep soaking tub.

OPPOSITE: Make the most of the shower in a bath remodel; it's where most people get their daily bathing experience.

The other school of thought is, it's totally up to the homeowners. Some people like consistency. For them, the above paragraph will suit them. Others will take to the idea of trying different things in different bathrooms. Now, rarely will owners of contemporary homes create traditional baths. So what this is really all about is whether a traditional home can have a contemporary bath. The answer is, if it's your home and you want it to, then yes. These are the schools of thought from which to choose.

What is the biggest misconception consumers have when they start redesigning their bathrooms?

Price! And time! Consumers have no idea how much a bath remodel really costs, because of home center advertisements.

If a home center advertises a low-end faucet, people come to a bath designer expecting a full remodel not to cost much. If the job is done right, the products will cost more than they will at the home center. A custom cabinet for a small space will cost more than a stock cabinet that's mass-produced on a line.

Time is a huge factor. It's a smaller room, but it can take almost as long as a kitchen. Bathrooms are labor intensive, as opposed to kitchens, which are product intensive. The same trades people have to go in there. Someone has to do electrical work in a small space and plumbing work in a small space. The bottom line is that labor can easily be three to four times the cost of the fixtures.

What trends do you foresee in bathroom design?

Aesthetics are very important, so look for more eye-catching safety items, such as grab bars that look nice. Also expect more appealing non-slip surfaces, like honed marble, and bathtubs that are easier to get into and out of. Drawer pulls are becoming more ergonomic so that an arthritic finger can get behind them.

Functional items are becoming more prevalent. Faucets are becoming easier to operate. They're being built higher up, and technology has been improved in an area known as proximity activation. In many airport faucets, for example, people wave their hands in front of an electronic eye, and the water flows. Recent technology aims to

ABOVE: Some say a contemporary bath shouldn't go in a traditional home. Ultimately, however, the homeowner has final say on the décor.

OPPOSITE: In a real-bath situation, this lav would need at least 15 inches of clearance from the center to either side—any extra clearance would be better.

ABOVE: The cabinets look swell, but more importantly, they provide lots of storage.

eliminate that eye. A device creates a magnetic field around the water supply lines below the faucet, and when someone approaches the faucet and interrupts the field, the valve opens up and water flows. That trend is really going to become popular in the bathroom because it will work on any style of faucet, whereas the old eye seemed limited to contemporary styles.

Other functional items to look for are showerheads that are easier to control and jetted tubs that control everything from a panel.

The bathroom is becoming a retreat instead of strictly a hygiene area. This has really started to take hold in more and more homes. The space can include a deluxe shower and a bigger bathtub, where one person is comfortable but two people can also fit. Kitchen amenities are starting to creep in, too: coffee makers, little refrigerators, bar sinks. Any bath with a little extra space can be turned into a retreat by adding a window and putting in a comfy chair. That way, a person can take a bath and maybe rest and read, and get a cup of coffee or a cold soda while drying her hair.

What is your advice on bathroom safety?

Plan for the future. Homeowners who may not need grab bars and don't want to put them in should at least provide the backing to put them in later. They may even want to purchase them now so that the finishes match and put them in the basement. Color contrast is important, too. Put contrasting color at the threshold of the shower. Make sure the space is lit well. Put a separate recessed light over the toilet and shower instead of relying on general lighting.

ABOVE: If the budget allows for luxury fixtures and décor, take the plunge.

Here's a way for relatively able-bodied people to gauge what physical adjustments they might want to make when remodeling their bathrooms: Do two hours of strenuous exercise—just blow out the body. Then go into the bathroom and go through a normal hygiene routine, using all the areas of the bathroom and all the fixtures. Take a shower. Sit in the tub when wet and try to get out. Sit on the toilet and get up. Turn the faucet on and off. These steps should provide some idea as to what areas of the bathroom require safety assistance.

Another safety issue in the bath comes from humidity. Get a big enough exhaust fan to regulate the humidity. Ventilation fans change the air in the room, and without that, mold and mildew develop inside of cabinets and right behind the baseboard molding. Bathrooms that are less than six years old can have mold damage. Once it

builds up, the damaged area has to be completely torn out. That costs more than getting a good exhaust fan.

What is your advice on luxury bathroom fixtures such as jetted tubs and luxury showers?

Anyone who has the money for it should go for it. People really get their money's worth out of a bathroom. It's one of the few rooms where they can pamper themselves. They can watch TV and relax. Empty nesters are turning kids' bedrooms into bathrooms. They're flipping their houses. Jetted tubs are a luxury, and they can be great. In luxury showers, people should make sure they have a seat and a grab bar to help get themselves up.

Keep in mind, however, that there are no bargains in luxury bathing fixtures. Two items might look the same, but on the less expensive one, either the surface is going to deteriorate quicker or something mechanical is going to fail quicker. For example, two showers might both have pressure balance or thermostatic valves, and one might be half the price of the other. Investing the money up front will pay dividends down the line, because the more expensive one won't conk out three or four years down the road. On average, to buy the cheaper one is to expect a lower lifespan. Yes, the manufacturer may provide a new cartridge for the lifetime of the fixture, but that still means going through the hassle of having a plumber replace it.

What bathroom innovations will have the most impact in the coming years?

The diameter of grab bars is mandated by federal law, and the current law is why grab bars look the way they look. If the

government changes the regulation, grab bars could still have the same function in terms of safety but with the potential for more diverse designs.

Expect more quartz in the bathroom, as opposed to natural products. Quartz requires less maintenance than stone. Manufacturers have finally gotten to a palette and a look that is more attractive and acceptable to a broader range of consumers. One manufacturer has unveiled a manmade granite quartz product that looks like concrete—with a very soft, subtle texture. It doesn't look like quartz.

Overall, the bathroom is becoming a multi-purpose room. People are even starting to put all-in-one washer/dryer units in the bathroom. They're adding all these bells and whistles to really pamper themselves. What's more, people are really buying quality. They want their remodeled baths to last. They're willing to spend a considerable amount more if they know it will last longer.

ABOVE: Two-sink bathrooms are great, if there's enough elbow room for both people.

LEFT: Look for classy touches that are practical, like this side-mounted towel bar.

OPPOSITE TOP: Jetted tubs come in standard sizes, too, for small bathrooms.

OPPOSITE BOTTOM: Hidden compartments provide elegant storage for various bathroom necessities.

Traditional Bathrooms

Home Completed

OPPOSITE: The centerpiece of this bath is an angled vanity with two undermount sinks and a green-marble top. The mirror reflects a 5-foot chest that makes the room function as a dressing room as well as a bath. Sunshine pours in through the new skylight and an awning window made of patterned acrylic.

BELOW: The seashell-shaped drawer pulls on the chest and elsewhere in the room are brass with a faux-iron finish.

COZIED UP AGAINST A LANDSCAPED COURTYARD, this 2,000-square-foot white stucco house had nearly everything its busy owners wanted: three bedrooms plus a loft-style office within barking distance of the Pacific Ocean in Seal Beach, California. What it lacked was a master bath that looked or worked as the owners desired.

They needed designer Dana Jones, of The Kitchen Consultant in nearby Long Beach, to address some major issues. Among these were that the tub was too big and the shower too small. They also regarded the middle of the room as so much wasted space. Jones soon realized the solution was to gut the space; to start all over and work within the existing space to bring the bathroom up to par with the rest of the home.

One of the key design moves, and the first one Jones made, was relocating the bathroom door. It had been on the wall directly across from the bed, which meant that a nighttime bathroom visitor flicking the light switch delivered a blast of light to the person trying to sleep—or worse, to the person already sleeping. The new sleeper-friendly doorway is positioned where the shower stall was in the old design. Jones created a vestibule by shifting the entryway about 6 feet to the left.

The new shower enclosure, twice the size of its cramped 3x3-foot predecessor, is angled behind the vanity in the center of the room. The tub and toilet stand in their original locations but have been significantly upgraded: The tub is now a whirlpool model that's surrounded by an elegant marble deck; the toilet occupies a room of its own, with a door for privacy.

Because the bathroom is so often bathed in sunlight, Jones chose soft colors: a cream tone for the painted walls, beige marble for the floor and tub backsplash. The only strong color is the green on the vanity counter, the tub deck and the diamond-like dots in the beige flooring.

The custom cabinets Jones specified for the bathroom are in keeping with this soothingly monochromatic scheme: traditional in style and warm in tone, with an elegant glazed finish. Doors and drawer fronts have raised panels, as does the front of the tub deck.

Raised paneling also highlights four of the 10 drawers on the 5-foot-tall chest that stands directly beyond the double vanity. Having an auxiliary chest

makes the space useful as a dressing room as well as a bath. This is especially helpful as the couple did not want to crowd the bedroom with dressers.

The husband said that although all of their home projects have turned out beautifully, for him, the bathroom was the real revelation. "It never occurred to me when I looked at the drawings that it would turn out so well."

WHAT MAKES IT WORK

THE DOORWAY was positioned so that a nighttime bathroom user doesn't disturb the bedroom sleeper.

THE OVERSIZE TUB and undersize shower were replaced with more modern models; the new tub is a standard whirlpool, and the marble-lined shower has a tile bench and ample elbow room.

BEIGE MARBLE flooring and tub backsplash replace milky-blue tile from the 1970s.

AN AWNING WINDOW over the tub replaces a hard-to-reach slider; the new window is translucent acrylic that provides privacy without cutting out natural light.

THE TOILET occupies a room of its own, closed off by a door to ensure complete privacy.

A 5-FOOT-TALL CHEST, opposite the vanity, eliminates the need for dressers in the master bedroom.

ABOVE: The marble-lined shower angles behind the vanity. Because of the placement of the spout and the height of the threshold, no protective door or curtain is needed to contain splashes.

RIGHT: Separating the shower and bathtub gives this space maximum flexibility when it comes to function.

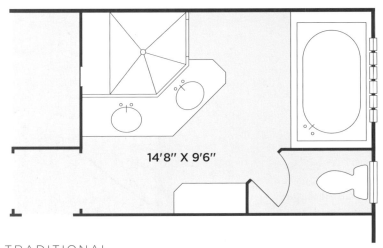

14'8" X 9'6"

RIGHT: The new toilet is exactly where the old one was, but now it is enclosed in its own room. The angle of the door echoes one section of the vanity.

BELOW: A band of wave-patterned mosaic ceramic tile, a reference to the nearby Pacific Ocean, was set into the beige marble backsplash that rises behind the sink faucets.

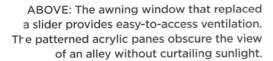

ABOVE: The awning window that replaced a slider provides easy-to-access ventilation. The patterned acrylic panes obscure the view of an alley without curtailing sunlight.

RIGHT: The tub features a handheld showerhead and a standard spout. The marble backsplash has a bullnose edge that's aligned with the line of the countertops.

Soaking Up Some Sky

SITTING IN THIS SECOND-STORY BATHTUB provides an experience in spaciousness, even if the room isn't exactly massive. For one thing, generous windows surround the whirlpool tub, ushering the outside in. For another, the ceiling keeps going up, up, up. Before the owners remodeled, none of this would have been possible.

When the longtime owners of this vintage house in central Toronto decided to build a kitchen/family room addition, they splurged and topped it with a second floor so they could have what they had always wanted: a separate master suite. The architect drew up plans for the addition, then bathroom designers Erica Westeroth and Tim Scott, of XTC Design in Toronto, went to work and ultimately made the 8½x10-foot master bathroom a special refuge.

The house was built in the early 1900s and had a traditional character. Nevertheless, the homeowners insisted on a contemporary look, according to Westeroth. Then again, they didn't want it to be so modern that it would be alien to the style of the house. To achieve that balance, the design team chose Carrara marble in a neutral tone and paired it with brass fittings that recall Victorian design.

Within a space that's modest for a master bath, the homeowners wanted the vanity, shower and tub to appear as separate elements. They also wanted the tub to be a huge corner whirlpool. These demands and a lush backyard that just begged for a view dictated tweaks in the architect's plans. Most notably, they moved the room's four windows to the corner, directly above the tub, immediately making that fixture a focus.

Although the plumbing fixtures are installed along the three walls facing the entry—a fairly standard arrangement—the ceiling treatment truly gives the space its surprising air of grandeur. The designers worked with the high ceiling, creating a stepped soffit with angles that follow the lines of the tub and shower. The ceiling is flat in the center of the room, and the stepped-up sections are along the periphery. Standing in the room, the eyes are drawn upward, first to the ceiling, then to the windows and the landscape beyond them. Privacy is a non-issue. Looking out, the only surroundings are trees and sky.

THE WAITING GAIN
Designer Erica Westeroth's clients lived in their old house for several years before expanding and remodeling it, and that experience paid off. Westeroth offers this advice:

STAY CALM People don't want to live in used houses, because they don't reflect their personalities. Things may not seem aesthetically pleasing or well laid out, but don't get too anxious. Resist the urge to remodel right away.

BE PATIENT It always helps to live in the house first so you can begin to understand how it functions, its limits, where the light comes in, where the best views are, etc.

GET REAL Only after you have lived in the house for a period of time will the changes you desire really start to reveal themselves to you.

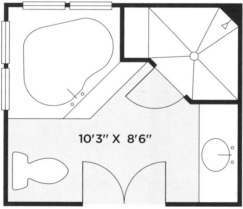

10'3" X 8'6"

PRECEDING PAGES: A marble deck, backsplash and steps create an elegant setting for the corner whirlpool tub. The designers altered the architect's original plan so all the windows would wrap around the tub.

ABOVE: The vanity, with four deep drawers and three shelves behind a tall cabinet door, has a single porcelain sink. Overhead lighting is complemented by a light strip, concealed by a valance directly under the cabinet.

OPPOSITE: The glassed-in enclosure, big enough for two, has a built-in bench plus a handheld shower as well as a fixed showerhead.

ABOVE: The symmetrical arrangement of elements and repositioned windows make the whirlpool tub a sunbathed corner of the bath.

ABOVE RIGHT: A pair of shell-shaped brass hooks for towels clings to the marble wall in the toilet niche.

RIGHT: Brass fittings, like this traditionally styled combination tub-filler and handheld shower, are in polished brass with white porcelain buttons and handles.

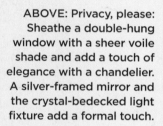

WINDOWS
AND SHADES

REINVIGORATING A BLAH BATHROOM can begin with the windows. Evoke the ambience of a mini-spa and shut out the world—but not the sunlight—with gorgeous windows and creative shades. It can make a world of difference. For more information on windows, you can refer to pages 140-141.

ABOVE: Privacy, please: Sheathe a double-hung window with a sheer voile shade and add a touch of elegance with a chandelier. A silver-framed mirror and the crystal-bedecked light fixture add a formal touch.

BELOW: Add charm and sparkle—not to mention privacy—with a glass-block window. A stylish Roman shade provides added flair and seclusion. Tuck the tub underneath in an unused corner to take advantage of the filtered light.

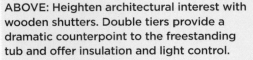

ABOVE: Heighten architectural interest with wooden shutters. Double tiers provide a dramatic counterpoint to the freestanding tub and offer insulation and light control.

OPPOSITE RIGHT: Step up to a sink that comes with a view outside! Capitalize on a corner nook with two windows that follow the ceiling lines. The result: a light-filled space that's functional and interesting.

TOP: Create a temple—surround a sunken white marble tub with Palladian windows and columns to capture the essence of a classical grotto. Gold-toned fixtures enhance the luxury.

ABOVE: Top down/bottom up honeycomb shades offer options for many configurations. Set into the frame, the uncluttered look doesn't obscure the window grid's appeal.

LEFT: Open up a top-floor bathroom to sun and air with a skylight. A half-wall of glass-block partitions off the shower area, allowing light from above to spread through the room but preventing water from doing the same.

Bathing Beauty

SUMPTUOUS MATERIALS AND ATTENTION TO DETAIL were behind the Cinderella-like transformation of this master bathroom from bare-bones basic to sparkling jewel. The story is a modern remodeling fairy tale.

Once upon a time, this bath in a 1980s Tudor-inspired home in New Jersey was boxy, bland and boring. The glorious potential of the room fell victim to a neutral color scheme and a layout that wasted floor space and ignored the space's inspirational possibilities in favor of the merely functional. It even had an ever-so-predictable tub/shower combination. The only source of natural light was one itty-bitty window that made the room feel even more drab and dreary, according to designer Jeannie Fulton, of Ulrich Inc. in Ridgewood, New Jersey.

Fulton devised solutions to let the space shine in a new light—literally. One of her first steps was to blast open the existing window in the bathroom to take advantage of the backyard view. The house has a fabulous swimming pool, and the family wanted to be able to see out over that area. With bold new expanses of glass, the bathroom is now flooded with natural light. Arched panes over the double windows function as an architectural element. This element finds an echo in the lowered ceiling of the bathing alcove, which consists of the whirlpool tub, recessed lights and built-in storage on both ends. Walls are painted a soothing blue-green, another primal step in Fulton's plan to take a very unattractive bathroom and make it a more luxurious and relaxing space. A crystal chandelier suspended from a recessed dome in the ceiling punctuates a major statement: this room is all about opulence, luxury and pampering.

Because most homeowners use their tubs not so much to bathe but more to unwind, Fulton added a glass-enclosed steam shower for everyday use. She created the shower area by knocking down two walls to the left of the entry and building into an area that previously had housed only heating and cooling ducts. One corner of the shower has its own built-in tiled bench, a feature that is convenient not only for sitting, but also for leg shaving. A mosaic border rims the bench wall and continues around the room. The design of the border is a pick-up from a tile medallion inset in the marble floor. This look, drawn from Italian antiquity, is another enchanting theme in the space. Opposite the shower, the vanity wall has been transformed into an Old World style dressing area. The curved-leg wash basin and vanity table feature reproduction mirrors and crystal sconces. The gracefully arched cabinets offer loads of new storage space, yet they look as though they have been part of the home for years. They provide still another dose of traditional elegance to transform this bath.

Oh, and the homeowners and bathroom lived happily ever after. The end.

OPPOSITE: Throughout the space, curves—a small dome carved out of the ceiling, arched windows and a circular floor medallion—add architectural grace.

ABOVE: Centered beneath the window and balanced by storage units at both ends, the tub is the focal point of the room.

RIGHT: This bath is luxurious not only in finishes and appointments, but also in its generous use of floor space.

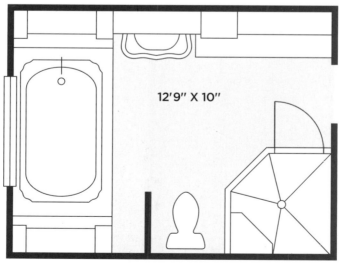

12'9" X 10'

OPPOSITE: Tucked into a niche between the tub and grooming station, the antique-style console sink and etched-glass mirror underscore the elegance that abounds in this bathroom.

MATERIAL MATTERS

Furniture-style detailing for cabinets and dramatic lighting choices add to the luxe look of this master bathroom.

FRENCH VANILLA MARBLE TOP counters are in the dressing area as well as the tub deck. Marble tiles of the same creamy tone grace the floor to create an open expanse. The polished stone offers a reflective surface that heightens the new sense of spaciousness in the room.

A CRYSTAL CHANDELIER seems weightless, not overbearing, in the light, bright setting, while crystal sconces bounce light off of the etched-frame mirrors.

CROWN MOLDING adds the illusion of depth and dimension. Classic details—carved leaf motifs, molding and panel insets—tie together the painted white cabinets, window frame and tub surround.

ABOVE: The floor mosaic is based on an Italian design.

LEFT: An expansive, well-lighted makeup area spoils its user with convenient storage.

OPPOSITE: Enclosing the shower in glass enhances the airy quality of the room.

ask the experts

When installing a steam shower in a master bath, do you need to make major changes in the existing plumbing or electrical systems?

The extent of the changes will depend on the existing capabilities of the room. If there is no dedicated electrical line with a ground fault circuit interrupter (GFCI), one will need to be installed to power the steam generator. The steam generator must be remotely located in the attic, the basement, a closet or in a vanity cabinet next to the shower. A plumber should be able to run a hot-water line to the shower from the line that feeds the sink faucet in the room. Vapor-protected lighting will also be required.

A Sanctuary for Two Humans

BEYOND THREE SHUTTERED WINDOWS of this home in the northern Chicago suburbs is a wildlife sanctuary. On the other side of those windows is a decidedly non-wild sanctuary for the home's two human inhabitants. What's more, it functions as two bathrooms, one for the husband and one for the wife.

Diane Bohstedt, of Insignia Kitchen & Bath Design, designed all the interiors in the home. The master bath became an extension of the other rooms she worked on with the homeowners. In particular, it picks up a lot from the kitchen, which has a similar color palette.

The essentially monochromatic scheme of the kitchen contributed greatly to the soothing ambience the owners wanted in the bath. They also desired style longevity, which is why they didn't pick funky colors or finishes; they wanted to make sure everything in the bathroom would remain current for years and years.

The room flows out of the master bedroom through a pair of tall wooden doors that can be swung shut for total privacy. The room measures approximately 15x12½ feet, with a 2-foot windowed bump-out behind the oversize whirlpool tub. The shower and tub are big enough for two, but the bath as a whole is segregated. The husband's side has a pair of small custom cabinets atop of a solid-surface countertop. Those cabinets rest at either end of the vanity and serve in lieu of the typical drawer unit to house toiletries.

The other far more elaborate side is for the wife. It consists of not only an angled vanity, but also clothing storage to the left of the sink, plus a dressing table and chair and beside them a tall cabinet for linens. Tying all of these elements together are cream-colored 12x12-inch ceramic tiles with terra-cotta and pale yellow diamond-shaped accents. To give the center of the tile floor some decorative punch, Bohstedt designed a "carpet" made of 6x6-inch tiles set on the diagonal and framed by the same border pattern that recurs throughout the room.

By the time Bohstedt became involved in this project, the house plan was pretty well set, so she and the homeowners worked within the established parameters. The master suite she designed is located on the first

SEPARATE YET EQUAL

The his-and-her separation is the most important aspect of this design, according to designer Diane Bohstedt. She feels most couples would want some sense of distinction. No matter how a shared bathroom is designed, you can customize it in terms of finishes as well as layout and accessories so that each person who uses the space experiences something special and exclusive.

Men and women both want privacy in the bathroom, Bohstedt says. Even in the smallest of baths, it really is possible to create some degree of separation.

PRECEDING PAGES: The "his" area beside the shower has a vanity fitted with a cupboard, drawers and small cabinets on the countertops. The homeowner wanted everything to have a place, with nothing left exposed.

ABOVE RIGHT: Hardware in the bath is brushed nickel with a distressed finish. It gives the room a lived-in feeling that belies its overall newness.

RIGHT: The his/her separation is evident in the floor plan, which features a toilet compartment with its own door and a "tile carpet" as the centerpiece.

FAR RIGHT: A premade tile border in terra-cotta, pale yellow and cream is a dominant decorating element.

floor of the home, separate from three upstairs bedrooms where the homeowners' family stays when visiting. Notwithstanding their love for their family, the master suite truly is a sanctuary.

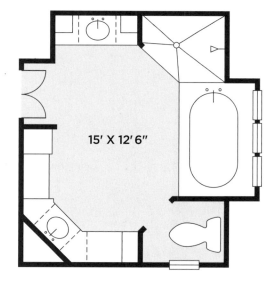

15' X 12' 6"

ask the experts

Is there a better way to clean the grout between ceramic wall and floor tiles than scrubbing it with a toothbrush?

Before you haul out the toothbrush, try spraying on and rinsing off a commercial grout-cleaning product or even a 50/50 bleach-and-water solution. Don't get bleach on metal components, however, home-care experts warn. It's liable to etch the metal.

If you need to scrub, use a nylon bristle brush, made for grout cleaning. (You'll find brushes at home-improvement stores.) Once the grout is clean, use a grout sealer to ward off stains and soap scum.

To spruce up grout, try a grout paint or colorant, also available at home-improvements stores or online. (Note: These are best used on glazed tile. Non-glazed tiles such as terra-cotta should be sealed first.) If the grout is cracking or missing in spots, replace it before water seeps behind tiles and damages walls.

OPPOSITE: A storage unit normally used in kitchen installations for holding wine bottles is deployed on the "her" side of the bath as a place for rolled-up towels.

FOLLOWING PAGE: A scalloped valance with tapered ends adds a soft touch to the light-filtering shuttered windows behind the tub. The birdhouse and bird figures allude to the wildlife sanctuary that is visible through the windows behind the house.

ADDING TEXTURE

Sleek is chic, but texture is better. Here's how to bring relief to a room: It's not difficult to add tactile appeal—be it actual roughness or mere simulation—to your bathroom. Follow the tips offered here to create a textured environment that visitors will want to run their fingers across.

ABOVE LEFT: These Spanish tiles recreate woven leather to provide a textured surface underfoot.

BELOW LEFT: Fields of bas-relief tiles create texture in two ways: framing a flush-mount mirror and defining a pedestal sink. These tiles offer quiet color and a strong pattern as well.

ABOVE: Layers of paint applied over a deliberately uneven coating of joint compound produce the look and feel of tree bark.

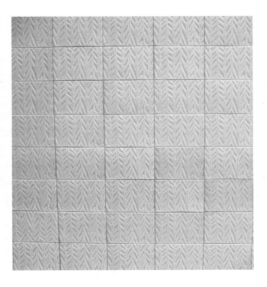

LEFT: These tactile tiles bring to mind leaves or perhaps feathers.

36 WAYS TO...
OPEN UP YOUR BATH

SOMETIMES A BATHROOM HAS TO STEAL SPACE from a closet or a bedroom to break out of its trapped-in feeling. Before hammers hit drywall, though, start smaller: Many simpler ways exist to visually expand a bath. Try light, color and trompe l'oeil tricks, and pay attention to decorative accessories. Also consider using transparent items—they add to the illusion of space by prompting the eyes to take in the entire room.

TOP: Use a clear-glass shower door to give the bathroom the illusion of size.

ABOVE: Continuous expanses of floor and wall tiles make a bath feel larger.

• Add white wainscoting and a narrow band of molding to the walls (about two thirds of the way up) to lift the eye upward, distracting attention from the size of the room.
• Paint walls and trim in a light, monochromatic color scheme.
• Give the illusion of depth by removing doors from cabinets and painting the interiors a lighter color.
• Choose ceramic tiles for walls and the floor in similar colors.
• Install a pedestal sink in place of a closed-in, boxy vanity cabinet.
• Hang double shower curtains to frame the tub enclosure; using a single curtain makes the space appear smaller.
• Replace a small window with glass blocks to take advantage of light without sacrificing privacy.
• Install a tubular skylight to add light and keep a windowless room from seeming like a dark cave.
• Cover one of the walls with mirrors to add a reflective surface.
• Take advantage of height: Hang an interesting piece of art under the peak of a roof or over a door.
• Store extra toiletries in a hallway linen closet to help keep the bathroom free from clutter.
• Install glass shower doors.
• Avoid window coverings altogether to lead the eye outside, but preserve your privacy by propping a small painting or two in front of an uncovered window.
• Hang a number of mirrors with simple frames over a vanity.

• Take advantage of spaces between wall studs: Install storage cubbies for towels rather than cluttering the room with them.
• Accentuate the height of the room by installing a border of colorful wallpaper near the ceiling.
• Emphasize vertical lines with a striped shower curtain.
• Invent a view by painting a window, complete with overflowing plant boxes, on one wall.
• Mount glass-topped knobs onto a piece of perforated board to hold towels, washcloths and bathrobes.
• Lighten up the proceedings with glass-shaded chrome lamps positioned on either side of a mirrored medicine cabinet to reflect and refract light.
• Keep window treatments simple and classic to make sure that they won't overwhelm the space.
• Store cotton balls and swabs, bath beads and other toiletries in clear-glass containers.
• Coax the eye upward by ringing the room with a border of small plates or china soap dishes.
• Install wallpaper with muted stripes to lengthen the room. Choose a small-figured overall print for the space when stripes might make the room appear too tall and narrow.
• Use transparent plastic chairs or cubes instead of dark wood or upholstered pieces that make the room look crowded.
• Provide both uplight and ambient light to make the room seem larger.

- Train a spot on one wall to create a bright expanse of light.
- Paint the ceiling sky-blue and accent it with wispy clouds.
- Replace wooden shelves on the wall with clear glass ones.
- Paint a mural on a wall to fool the eye into looking outward toward the "horizon."
- Splurge on a glass wash basin.
- Reduce intrusions that "shrink" the space. Remove all protruding objects, such as hanging shelves and towel racks.
- Reflect light off shiny surfaces.
- Expand the room horizontally: Use white or off-white solid surfacing for integral vanity sinks, as these colors won't interrupt the flow.
- Brighten and lighten up the room by replacing dingy linoleum flooring with bright, white tiles.
- Choose exposed shelving instead of hemmed-in storage containers; it won't overpower a small space.

ABOVE RIGHT: A white bath and shower module like this one coordinates with tile and flooring; light colors expand the space.

ABOVE: Acrylic- or glass-block windows like these add light but don't sacrifice privacy.

RIGHT: A vanity with an open shelf underneath, like this one, can help prevent a closed-in look and maintain visual flow.

Royal Retreat

OPPOSITE: Two console sinks beneath mirrored medicine cabinets make this design comfortable for sharing. A towel radiator sits outside the all-tile open shower.

A PROTOTYPE DREAM BATH, designed for Sarah Ferguson and with her help, is a beautiful private spa, a haven of pure relaxation. The Duchess of York, once married to England's Prince Andrew, second son of Queen Elizabeth, is a mother of two and an international spokesperson for Weight Watchers.

For her, bathroom luxury means a huge freestanding tub on its own platform, a doorless walk-in shower big enough for two—with a sizable bench—and a comfortable chair to relax in after bathing. She worked with interior designer Ingrid Leess to outfit this display bathroom with everything she would want in a pampering retreat.

Although the Duchess had an extensive wish list, Leess brought her design talent to bear. To complete the picture, the designer added a 26-inch television that disappears behind mirrored glass when not in use, plus a drawer refrigerator as part of a fully stocked refreshment center. The toilet and bidet are in their own separate space, behind a discreet pocket door.

In this hypothetical wonderland, the Duchess would lounge on a Queen Anne-style armchair with decorations by interior designer Katherine Stephens and wood finishing by James Matar. Three shades of wood stain, plus a special walnut wood finish and clear lacquer, define the chair. A small table, decorated in the same stains, patterns and motifs, completes a soothing setting for an after-bath tea beside an expansive picture window.

Leess wanted a serene feeling in a sophisticated space. The Duchess' preference for shades of blue motivated the choice of Italian tile in the shower. Her sense of whimsy prompted Leess' use of a wallpaper with butterfly motifs in the toilet compartment. As the Duchess wanted high visibility for most bath essentials, Leess placed colorful towels—some all cotton, some made of a very soft bamboo fiber/cotton mix—on open shelves. Two wall-hung towel radiators make the display beautiful.

Because of the Duchess' traditional leanings, the design team chose recessed-panel cabinets in pale maple, with leaf and flower accents etched into door borders. The cabinet hardware has a rustic brass finish. Extending the room's subtle natural theme, 24x24-inch Italian floor tiles that look and feel like bamboo complement a luscious leaf-patterned wallpaper.

Over all, the balance of hidden and seen bath essentials adheres to the Duchess' admonition, "No clutter, please." To broaden the appeal of the space, however, Leess added contrast—sconce lights, mirrored cabinets and console sinks with a decidedly contemporary look. There are shelves for toiletries—both open and tucked behind glass doors—and plenty of closed cabinets to keep items out of sight. Between the shower and the toilet compartment stands the bath's principle storage unit, a massive piece of furni-

RIGHT: A toilet and bidet (not shown) occupy a small room that can be isolated by a pocket door.

DESIGN CUES

• Separate areas for shower and toilet/bidet make this a plausible spa bath for two.
• Including a chair and table underscores this bath's design as a relaxation zone.
• Decorative sconce and chandelier lighting add touches of warmth and elegance.
• Mounted behind a two-way mirror, the TV becomes visible only when needed.

ture with seeded glass in some upper doors. There is shelving for towels and beauty aids, plus drawers and closed cabinets. Another cabinet shares space with the toilet and bidet, making that room even more practical.

In the super-size shower, the tile resembles a waterfall of blues, according to the designer, who collaborated on the many tile choices with Kevin Mashia, in consultation with the Italian Trade Commission/Ceramic Tiles of Italy. All of the design team's decisions were made with an eye to realizing the Duchess' vision of luxury. To put it another way, the space has a definite feminine feel to it.

ABOVE: A built-in bench extends between adjustable sprays on two walls of the shower stall. Inset into ceramic tile walls are glass tiles in stripes. Nearby, a towel hangs on a wall-hung towel warmer, available in electric or hydronic models.

ask the experts

I've fallen in love with the look of stand-alone clawfoot tubs. Are there any special plumbing requirements or concerns involved with installing them?

As long as the bathroom has plumbing to accommodate a tub, any concerns regarding clawfoot or other freestanding tubs should be minor. Everything needed to convert from a built-in to a freestanding tub is readily available, and a professional plumber should know how to make the conversion. Although plumbing access from the floor is preferable, freestanding tubs can take faucets that run from the wall. Before making a buying decision, wise shoppers will have a professional check out their bathroom plumbing and advise them about their options.

ABOVE: The freestanding soaking tub is deeper and longer than standard. It sits on a tub base, as opposed to legs.

OPPOSITE: A tall hutch, with drawers as well as seeded glass and solid doors, can hold most bathroom necessities. A wall-mounted intercom system ensures convenient communication.

ABOVE: Concealed behind the mirror is a 26-inch TV visible only when the set is on. A drawer refrigerator makes it possible to enjoy cold drinks here as well as hot tea.

Graceful End to a Rough Sport

IN THE OLD DAYS, EVERY MORNING in the Blombach bathroom of this 1885 brownstone was like hockey night in Boston. "Twenty-seven years ago when my husband, Michael, and I were first married, we were constantly hip-checking each other out of the way," Jackie Blombach says. Thankfully, they figured out a solution on their own. "We've had two sinks ever since." Now, after a professional remodel, the tasteful master bath in Jackie and Michael's condo seems much too civilized for any such brusque maneuvers.

On the opposite end of the closeness spectrum, whoever wanted to take a shower suddenly turned into the vanishing spouse. "When we moved in, the master bath had a very large spa tub, but no shower," Jackie says. "We would take our showers across the hall in the guest bath, which didn't make sense."

Here again, they came up with an idea. "We decided to do away with the tub and replace it with a large steam shower," Jackie says. "Winters here can be very drying. We have a forced-air heating system, and it's nice to use the steam shower to give relief to your nose and lungs, especially when you have a cold."

Jackie, who works in the historic preservation field, wanted a modern bath that echoed the past and the brownstone's pedigree. Working with Jason Simonetty, of Lee Kimball Kitchens in Boston, she chose honed limestone for the shower walls, counters and backsplash. She preferred its soft matte finish. The shower floor of tumbled marble mosaic tile provides good traction along with beauty and durability.

Simonetty designed the vanity to hold the all-important double sinks, adding traditional details such as raised-panel doors and a cut-out, furniture-esque toekick. Above the vanity, a custom-made mirrored medicine chest is set into the wall. This configuration provides deep storage without protruding awkwardly over the sinks.

A cherry armoire at one end of the room repeats details of the painted vanity cabinets and offers pleasing contrast with its dark finish. Towels and linens reside in the armoire's top half; the bottom is organized like a kitchen pantry, with easily accessible shelves in the doors.

PRECEDING PAGES: A transom above the shower door, normally kept open, is closed when it's time for steam. The steam generator is hidden in the built-in shower bench and is accessible from a closet in an adjoining room.

DOUBLE FEATURES

STEPPING BACK the stacks of drawers in the base cabinets at either end of the vanity creates a unit with a more attractive, less bulky profile. This is particularly important in small rooms, where massive cabinets can overwhelm the space.

THE CUSTOM-MADE CHERRY ARMOIRE was given a moisture-resistant finish, but the designer emphasizes the importance of good ventilation in a bath with wood cabinets, especially when a room has no operable windows, as is the case in this design.

THE DESIGNER SAYS he wanted the vanity and medicine cabinet to give the impression of being distinct pieces of furniture, especially as they are visible from the master bedroom. Envision and anticipate how the space will unfold as it is viewed from any adjoining area; just looking at a design on paper doesn't capture this perspective.

ABOVE RIGHT: On the wall opposite the sinks, two wicker laundry baskets slide out from beneath a built-in bench.

ABOVE: A handheld personal sprayhead is the perfect accessory for a steam shower installation, letting users cool down on demand.

RIGHT: The matte finish of the limestone counters and backsplash evokes a time-worn look appropriate to the 19th-century building.

BRIGHTEN THE BATH

Making a splash in the bath can be as easy as changing the paint on the walls and unleashing a little imagination. The sky's the limit: Bathrooms have no hard-and-fast rules for colors. Here are a few handy tips to keep in mind before that first paintbrush gets loaded up:

THINK OF THE BATHROOM AS A BACKDROP. Whatever color the bathroom takes will reflect on all its users' skin when they look in the mirror. For this reason, warm tones such as creams, pinks and red tones, are customary in bathrooms where people primp in the morning. Cool greens and blues can work, however, in bathrooms that serve different purposes—powder rooms, for instance. Many might find watery tones reflect off the skin and detract from their appearance, even though they make a bathroom look fabulous.

USE BOLD COLORS IN SUBTLE WAYS. Taking the plunge from a beige bathroom to a brighter one doesn't have to be drastic. Layer four or five colors for a soft, sophisticated effect. Softer midtones can mute strong tones for a more subtle look. In addition, these techniques work wonders in small bathrooms. Layering colors or using glazing products can enlarge the feel of the space and also soften the impact of the wall surface, giving the room an airy, ethereal look.

MAKE A STATEMENT. With do-it-yourself kits and home-improvement TV shows to inspire them, homeowners have embraced arts and crafts. To make one-of-a-kind statements, they have turned to such strategies as appliqués and stenciling. These techniques give a touch of playfulness to bathrooms. When a design moves upward on the wall, it also takes away from the harshness of the ceiling line. With a little creativity, a bathroom can go from plain and utilitarian to dreamy and romantic.

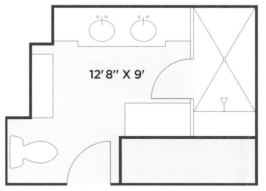

12' 8" X 9'

ABOVE: Centrally located in the room—equally convenient to the shower and the vanity area—an armoire crafted of cherry holds towels and toiletries.

LEFT: Once a large but rarely used bathtub was removed, the new layout of the room fell into place. A spacious steam shower scaled to accommodate two people is the anchor to the space.

As Good as Old

OPPOSITE: A lowered section of countertop acts as a subtle border between the two basins; the change in levels keeps clutter from migrating too far toward the "wrong" side of the vanity. This also allows the center mirror to expand a few inches to fill the extra wall space.

BELOW: The faucets are a contemporary stainless steel interpretation of a classic cross-handled design.

DESPITE THEIR AESTHETIC CHARMS, bathrooms designed 70 years ago are functionally prehistoric; they should have dinosaur bones in them. But for the past 25 years, homeowners Mary and John Lee (and their two daughters, now grown) successfully overlooked the shortcomings of the upstairs bath in their home in Chevy Chase, Maryland, and managed to share the space. Now that the family has grown to include visiting grandchildren, the Lees decided it was time to add a small but classy master bath for their own personal use while updating the former room for guests.

Instead of a bath that immediately tipped itself off as being brand-new, the couple worked with Cynthia McClure, of Grossmueller's Design Consultants in Washington, D.C., to create a design that appeared as if it could have been uncovered in some archaeological dig of the original 1935 Cape-style home. "We didn't want anything too grand or fussy," says Mary, admitting aesthetics played an important role in the overall design scheme. "It had to be luxurious but fit within the context of our old house."

Despite the modest size, the 180-square-foot addition manages to accommodate everything on the Lees' wish list. The dressing area features his-and-hers sinks made of creamy Carrara marble (a material that was commonly used in homes and commercial buildings throughout the 1920s and 1930s, Mary says), a handsome mirror-topped vanity and a built-in ironing board cleverly recessed in the cavity between wall studs. Clean-lined cabinets with brushed-nickel knobs convey a Shaker-like simplicity. Cherry wood in the cabinets underscores the warm honey-colored oak floor. The radiator tucked beneath a window was specifically refurbished to give the appearance "that it's been there forever," says Mary.

A few steps away the designer specified a shower room that evokes a spa-like feeling. McClure managed to squeeze all the necessary amenities into the relatively small space, plus she made room for a bidet, which Mary had asked for. Overall, the room has a very clean look that's classic, functional and essentially free of curves.

The light-filled space is a calm oasis thanks to a palette of monochromatic materials. Walls tiled in dove-gray and arctic-white replicate the look of traditional wainscoting. Towels and other assorted bath

accoutrements are stowed above on a sturdy wall-length shelf where they can be easily accessed.

After sharing a communal space for so many years, Mary is pleased to finally have a place to relax and get dressed without anyone pounding on the door. "I don't know how I ever managed before," she says with a laugh.

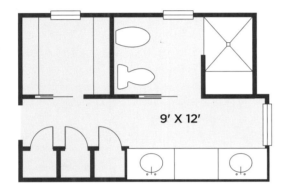

9' X 12'

ABOVE: Locating the shower away from the sinks avoids foot-traffic tie-ups. Because clearance was an issue, the shower room has pocket doors. A radiant heating system keeps the granite-tiled floor warm underfoot.

OPPOSITE: This towel bar and mirror are just outside the shower. Placing the toilet and shower by themselves relieves congestion in the small room without crowding the fixtures.

LEFT: Mary insisted on a bidet—a concession to her European upbringing. To stretch storage space, folded towels are kept on a wall-length shelf convenient to the shower.

ABOVE: The simple perimeter tile treatment continues around the walls of the shower stall, attractively blending it

FEATURES FOR TWO

Consider the following suggestions when planning a bath for two:

POSITION HIS-AND-HERS SINKS at opposite ends of the room, rather than right next to one another. This will help eliminate elbow bumping and allow privacy for each user.

INSTALL AN ADJUSTABLE SHOWERHEAD with a handheld spray that can accommodate different heights. This probably would be useful to most households. (Mary is 5 foot 3, her husband is 6 feet.)

INCORPORATE A BENCH in the shower—ideally, one big enough to comfortably seat two people.

DESIGNATE SPECIFIC DRAWERS, shelves and closet spaces for each person who will be using the bath. In addition to separate drawers designed for toiletries and grooming items, Mary and John each have their own wardrobe and shoe closet.

36 WAYS TO ADD ELEGANCE TO YOUR BATH

AS IN THE FASHION REALM, elegance in the home takes its cues from styles that are timeless. Look for graceful lines, luxurious details and classic designs to add refinement to your bath, and choose from the following tips.

- Install a lavatory table or crystal sink.
- Surround the mirror with a gilded frame.
- Use a mirrored tray and etched-glass accessories to display toiletries.
- Trim guest towels with elegant gold bullion fringe or lace trim.
- Replace ordinary tub and sink hardware with an exotic gold-colored set.
- Indulge in orchid plants to create the ambience of a deluxe spa.

- Install clear-resin towel racks.
- Fill wall-mounted glass vases with flowers—fresh or faux.
- If space allows, provide a place to lounge with a terrycloth-covered chaise.
- Cover the walls with a striated silk-like wallpaper for a high-end look.
- Hang a lace shower curtain.
- Add opulence with thick, luxurious towels.
- Loop strands of faux pearls and rhinestones around a mirror.
- Brighten up the space with wall-mounted crystal sconces.
- Surround a shower with a glass-block wall.
- Drape panels of delicate lace on either side of a window.
- Treat feet to soft surfaces in the bath with thick chenille rugs.
- Create ambience throughout the room by installing dimmer switches.
- Provide a tray of pillar candles for bathing by candlelight.
- Roll up extra towels and tie them with satin ribbons. They look chic either stacked up or filling a basket.
- Drop a sink into an ebony-painted vintage dresser accented with gold or silver.
- Hang your shower curtain with sparkling glass or stainless hooks.
- Paste a frieze of mirrored tiles around the room to create an elegant border. Edge it with gold or silver cord.
- Stencil the walls with a stylized Oriental design motif in gold.
- Hang up framed black-and-white photographs or architectural drawings.
- Cover a light fixture with a lampshade made from capiz shell.
- Repurpose a vintage sink stand. Position it next to the tub to hold soaps and other bathing necessities.

BELOW: Thick, textured towels add impressive opulence.

58

RIGHT: Monogrammed linens provide that luxury-hotel demeanor.

BELOW RIGHT: Glass and beaded shower hooks can add sparkle to a bathroom.

BELOW: A vintage sink stand recalls the elegance of days gone by.

- Sew a Roman shade in crushed velvet or silk for the window.
- Buy a sleek steel bathroom trolley table with glass shelves.
- Choose wall tiles that have a glossy finish for a shimmering effect.
- Have a marble slab cut to cover the top of the vanity for an old-fashioned look.
- Monogram your shower curtains.
- Tuft the walls with white chintz and tiny silver studs.
- Canopy the tub with gauzy netting draped over a wooden coronet suspended from the ceiling.
- Affix decorative molding to a simple wooden chair. Paint the chair white and gild the wood molding.
- Check out yard and garage sales for vintage knickknacks that can bring a classic look when arrayed on a shelf.

Eclectic
Bathrooms

How Blank Slate Becomes Marble

DESIGNER SUSAN WATERS STARTED with a blank slate. Her client doubled the size of his 100-year-old farmhouse in Wayne, Illinois, a leafy Chicago suburb, adding nearly 2,000 square feet. As part of the expansion, he asked her to conjure a master bath to please modern, eclectic tastes, and respect the home and its woodsy 7-acre property. One specific request was that she use marble; exactly how was up to Waters, a National Kitchen and Bath Association member based in Barrington, Illinois.

Concluding that sharp edges and shiny surfaces would fit poorly in pastoral surroundings, Waters chose warm-hued, honed marble for the floor, walls and tub surround. She had the top of the backsplash cut into a distinctive free-form contour for a natural, more organic look. The vanity counter complements this treatment: The front edge is 3 inches thick, thanks to a triple-layer buildup of stone. The fabricator then chiseled the edge for a rough texture that suggests the look of natural rock. The vanity top and tub deck—a lighter, creamy Bottachino marble—are the only polished stone in the bath.

Waters struggled to come up with mirrors that she felt didn't obscure the beauty of the stone walls. After considering numerous solutions, she suspended frameless mirrors from slim steel cables. An antique armoire to the right of the vanity holds items that would normally go in the medicine cabinet that Waters' mirror precluded. Bringing antique furniture into this contemporary setting is characteristic of the decor of the house as a whole, which displays a variety of old and antique pieces that have been set against what the homeowner calls a "minimalist" backdrop.

The frameless glass shower emphasizes how open the 156-square-foot room is. The stripped-down fixtures nevertheless offer luxurious options. The shower has a 12-inch rainfall showerhead, handheld sprayer and three adjustable body sprays; the tub has forced-air jets.

If the homeowner had it to do over, he'd change one thing. "I'd heat the floor," he says, "because the marble gets cold in the winter. There's a large crawl space underneath, so at some point, we'll probably go ahead and do it." It's a lesson learned, but other than that, he's thrilled with the majestic marblescape that sprang from a completely blank slate.

PRECEDING PAGES: The shower enclosure boasts many essentials and options, from a shaving mirror to a built-in bench to an adjustable hand spray. A glass partition lets the sun in.

RIGHT: Externally plumbed rainfall showerheads like this one prevent opening up the ceiling—something overhead designs often require.

BELOW: Metal serves as a machine-made counterpoint to dominant natural marble.

BOTTOM: Most of the fittings are curved—a graphic reference to the flow of water.

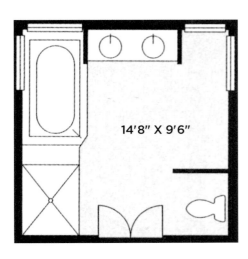

14'8" X 9'6"

LEFT: Double doors give the bath a grand entrance. The placement of fixtures around the perimeter of the room maximizes the amount of open space.

GOOD IDEAS

SIGHT SPECIFICS: If the bath has pleasant outdoor views, consider using natural materials and textures to bring the outdoor feeling inside.

CRYSTAL CLEAR: Designer Susan Waters recommends coating tempered-glass shower enclosures with auto-care products every few months and using a squeegee after showering to minimize water spots.

AIR STREAM: The tub Waters installed in this bathroom uses air jets to produce a hycromassage effect. Because no water flows through the tub's air channels, the jets will not clog. The owner can use any bath products he desires.

ROCK'S ROLE: Building up the edge of the vanity with a triple thickness of marble gives the stone a look of imposing heft. The fabricator then chiseled the edge of the counter to roughen up the texture and hide the seams where the layers join together.

ABOVE: The designer decided to hang the mirrors slightly away from the wall to show off the marble tiles. Steel cables support the mirrors from the ceiling.

LEFT: A stack of three marble slabs forms this counter. A fabricator's chisel brings out the stone's natural beauty and adds visual and tactile texture.

One Size Fits All

A SWARMING URBAN TRAFFIC HUB and most mornings in the second-floor bathroom of this five-bedroom Ridgewood, New Jersey, home are essentially the same thing. The family includes six children. When the homeowners decided to remodel the bath, they called in designer Tess Giuliani to make the space more livable and a tad less harrowing. Respectful of the English Cottage style of the 75-year-old home but eager to give a neglected room new life, Giuliani started by selecting warm, inviting colors and creating a design that maximized the 6x9-foot space.

All the new fixtures—sink, toilet, tub/shower—are exactly where their predecessors were. The walls are in their original locations as well. Nevertheless, choosing a sophisticated mix of tones and textures enabled the to designer endow this small space with an expanded sense of importance. The new tub went into an existing niche, which was finished in 4x4-inch tumbled-marble tiles in a subtle oatmeal tone.

Because of all the traffic, Giuliani designed a shallow vanity, counting on a tall cabinet near the door to handle storage of towels, linens, grooming gear and bathroom essentials. A copper vessel sink rests on top of a trapezoidal custom vanity with a slate top that angles back toward the wall. At a height of only 30 inches, the vanity is ideal for younger family members. Higher slate shelves embedded in the wall are specially designed for the older children's convenience.

The designer envisioned having a free-floating mirror above the vanity. So she drew a shape on the wall, and Butch Sietsma, who did the installation work and built all the cabinets, made a template. Sietsma cut a mirror to fit his template and carved into the drywall about half an inch so the mirror would be flush—with no protruding or reflecting edges. Sietsma also pruned limbs from his own birch trees to frame the mirror. The supports for the frame (but not the mirror) are straps that hang from railroad ties, hammered into the wall. Similar limbs also frame the window.

The family gave complete design license to Giuliani. Her instructions were to "look around the house; you will know what we want." She saw the texture and natural elements that characterized each room, and she grasped their personal style. She recognized that the house is earthy, with a sense of fun. The home is family-friendly, and with Giuliani's help, this bathroom is, too.

ABOVE: Room dimensions remained the same, but the designer freed up space by replacing the linen closet with a custom cabinet that's shallow at 24 inches deep and set back slightly from the edge of one of the tub walls.

ABOVE RIGHT: The storage cabinet, custom-built by carpenter Butch Sietsma, is designed to hold towels and linens. The door fronts are alternating raised and recessed maple boards coated with an oak stain.

RIGHT: The outdoors-inspired floor is made of matte-finish pebbles set on 12x12-inch sheets of mesh. After the sheets are trimmed to fit, thinset mortar and then grout are applied, creating a smooth, white background.

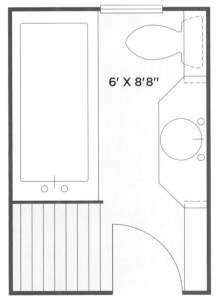

6' X 8'8"

ABOVE: Dark gray slate is cantilevered beyond both sides of the 30-inch-tall vanity cabinet to provide elbow room without crowding the space. Free-floating shelves on both sides of the vanity sit higher for older children. The vessel-style sink is copper.

WHAT MAKES IT WORK?

A FOUR-DOOR CABINET with 24-inch-deep adjustable shelves holds more gear than the traditional linen closet it supplants.

TILE AND WALL SURFACES feature soft tones with textured looks, far more serene than the harsh blue wall and floor tile they replaced.

THE VANITY IS SHALLOW, leaving ample walking space for equally ample family bathroom traffic.

WORK SURFACES ARE STAGGERED—some high, some low—to accommodate users of varying heights.

BIRCH LIMBS framing the mirror and window add a rustic accent to a room once bereft of style.

DIMINUTIVE DESIGNS

NOT LONG AGO, HAVING LIMITED BATHROOM space meant having limited design options. Once a full sink and a standard-size toilet went in, the leftover room would scarcely hold a single shelf, let alone a storage cabinet or—gasp!—a bathtub. Recently, though, designers have been taking on tiny rooms with fresh eyes, creating products with tight quarters in mind. And although these new products may be small in size, they are big on style, so even the most spatially deprived bathrooms can have perfect proportions and distinctive design at the same time.

ABOVE: This 17-inch angular toilet tucks neatly into a corner, eliminating dead space. This model is available in white and 10 more colors.

ABOVE: Products with multiple functions can be real space stretchers. This unit, for example, does double-duty by combining a tall, narrow storage cabinet and a basin in one unit. It measures 17 3/8 x 17 1/4 x 28 1/2 inches.

LEFT: Freestanding soaking tubs, such as this stainless steel model, can work great in undersize bathrooms. They deliver the total tub experience, but they take up a mere fraction of the space of a standard built-in bathtub.

LEFT: Because of the cantilevered design of this lavatory, it has the capacity of a full-size basin, but it requires less than half the countertop depth compared to a standard drop-in sink.

BELOW: This custom-made Japanese-style stainless steel soaking tub has a bench seat and a whirlpool system.

MIDDLE: This wall-mounted toilet takes up zero floor space and, with its hidden tank, minimal wall space.

OPPOSITE ABOVE RIGHT: This bathtub comes in right- or left-hand models.

OPPOSITE BELOW RIGHT: This wall-mounted sink measures just 23⅝ x 14 inches and is available in right-hand or left-hand versions, offering a bit of shelf space for baths of every configuration.

ABOVE: This corner bathtub is surely too large for tight quarters, isn't it? Not necessarily—it's big enough for two people, but it still fits into a relatively small space: 60x60x20¼ inches.

RIGHT: In another case of compact sophistication, this no-frills sink requires neither pedestal nor countertop.

A Second Thought, Set in Stone

CHICAGO IS BILL AND CONNIE SCHEY'S kind of metro area. It's where they live, and it's where Connie makes her living as a kitchen and bath designer at Insignia Kitchen & Bath Design Group in suburban Barrington, Illinois. After one too many winters in the Windy City, the couple purchased a second home, a small waterfront condominium in Sarasota, Florida. The condo boasted stunning vistas, but its interior hadn't been touched in at least 50 years.

Connie reconfigured the layout of the entire place, removing some interior walls to expose breathtaking beach and water views. In the process, she also brought a hopelessly outmoded kitchen and lackluster baths up to speed.

The catch was, the Scheys' new home was in a 10-story building. Connie could move the walls, but the water lines weren't going anywhere, and that made the bath renovations—in particular the 49-square-foot guest space off the foyer—daunting tasks.

Connie made the cramped quarters feel more spacious by replacing the bathtub with a slim, glass-enclosed shower stall. She also exchanged the standard-issue vanity for an eye-catching marble column topped with a stone bowl. "It's the first thing everyone notices," she says.

The second and third things must be the tremendous gash of marble that angles up the wall and the torn-edge mirror that hangs above the vanity. Perhaps all the roughness is a nod to the Chicago winter. Regardless, the character creates a first-rate small bathroom.

OPPOSITE: Strong diagonal lines and shiny surfaces distract from the small size of the space.

BELOW: A stone vessel sink sits atop a craggy cast pedestal base.

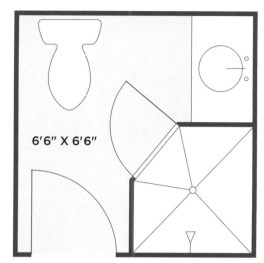

6'6" X 6'6"

ABOVE: Water lines in the 10-story building couldn't be redirected, so much of the work on this bathroom was cosmetic. The plan jettisons a space-hogging bathtub in favor of a comfortable shower.

LEFT: With the pedestal-style sink offering no additional storage, a simple wall-mounted cabinet keeps some basic toiletries at hand.

BELOW: Picking up on the rough-hewn motif throughout the bathroom, even the mirror has a jagged coastline.

OUTDOORS INSIDE
- Display a stunning orchid in a tole cache pot.
- Press ferns and frame them for a powder room wall.
- Be playful and make a shower curtain from fabric featuring swaying palm tress and hula dancers.
- Add a touch of the tropics to a bath with planters filled with bamboo.
- Capture the beauty of old roses with framed botanical prints.
- Make sachets of dried lavender or verbena and tuck them between folded towels.
- Use a scallop shell as a sea-worthy soap dish.
- Tuck pressed flowers or pieces of colorful beach glass in the pockets of a sheer shower curtain.
- Decorate hand towels with a border of tiny seashells.
- Make a dramatic frame for a bathroom mirror with a shell border.
- Create your own distinctive potpourri from the flowers and herbs in your garden.
- Border white towels with strips of moss-green linen.

LEFT: The bathroom floor is a light Jerusalem stone tile—the same material used for floors throughout the home; the walls are a dark Emperador marble. The contrast in colors, says Connie Schey, makes the walls appear to recede.

A NATURAL FIT

Designer Connie Schey offers advice on making natural stone surfaces work for you:

HANDLE WITH CARE. Some stones—especially softer varieties like marble and limestone—will stain. Those for whom staining is a concern should opt for a sturdier variety, such as granite, which stands up to far more abuse.

MIX AND MATCH. When it comes to combining stones, there are no rules. If it satisfies the homeowner's tastes, it's good.

WATCH THE WALLET. Because no two tiles are identical, stone must be installed over a more costly mud base.

AVOID HARSH CLEANSERS. Orange- and lemon-scented cleansers contain acids that can eat away at stone. Instead, stick to tried-and-true soap and water.

LIGHT AND EASY

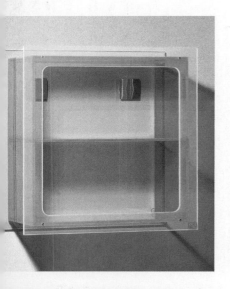

REMEMBER THE "ROY G BIV" ACRONYM from elementary school science class? Well, fifth graders generally don't learn a ton about how those pure colors of the light spectrum (red, orange, yellow, green, blue, indigo and violet) turned into the basis for chromatherapy, a branch of holistic healing that attempts to use color to affect health. Its practitioners believe that colored rays have an affect on the body: When a color is seen, it can have an emotional impact—but it may trigger an even more powerful physical reaction. When rays shine close to the body, the thinking goes, they penetrate it, travel through it, causing changes in cells, blood vessels, and the nervous system. Chromatherapy theory has even made its way into the design of bathroom fixtures and fittings.

Advances in light-emitting diode (LED) technology have enabled the creation of smaller, more affordable light systems that can change colors in succession—randomly and in patterns. The bath is an obvious staging area for chromatherapy, because small streams of color can be shone through either standing or running water, where their hues diffuse with enhanced intensity. Bathtubs, shower systems and sinks now offer chromatherapy options. When the water lights up with color, it gives off such a glow that designers—and many consumers—immediately fall in love. Laura Bohn, a New York–based interior designer, created a tranquil, Asian-influenced setting for a concept room in a manufacturer's design center. Her design features a model of the company's soaking tub that overflows with chromatherapy features. She says most people find the chromatherapy experience rather uplifting.

Uplifting beauty is one of the main attributes of another manufacturer's line of chromatherapy vessel sinks, which are crafted of a heat-proof crystal. The above-counter basins are crafted in Israel by a master glass artist in a variety of patterns. Each sink rests on a narrow ring that houses the LEDs, which glow in one of six colors that change depending on the temperature of the water pouring into the basin. The color disperses throughout the glass vessel and gives off a glow that is quite dramatic, especially in a darkened room.

Putting light into a glass sink probably sounds easier than it is, according to an executive at a sink manufacturer, but he claims no company had done it before. Having developed the ring concept, his firm then had to embed a temperature sensor in the crystal. Whatever the technology, the sink definitely picks up the chromatherapy trend that had begun in tubs and showers.

At least one major American manufacturer is also on top of this trend, offering a soaking tub and a line of six whirlpools, all with six-color chromatherapy lights in the walls of the units. Chromatherapy isn't cheap, though. The least expensive color-light whirlpool tub is around $3,000; the most expensive is more than $7,000.

The color-therapy concept ultimately derives from services offered by spas. Bohn sees spa products as a general trend in the bath. "These days, many people want spa-quality features in their own bathrooms," she says. "They want customized layouts and showers outfitted with lots of options for relaxation. Aside from the spa aspect, bathrooms are becoming more like living rooms— building luxury into them seems natural, not overindulgent." Another company adds thermo-massage along with chromatherapy. It advises relaxing in the tub with a color of choice in 15-minute sessions, concentrating on color entering the body.

Another available spa-style hydro treatment comes in the form of an electric light showerhead, which emits colors from fiber-optic sources embedded in 270 spray channels. Homeowner Ken Green, of David, Florida, was one of the first to own this particular amenity. Although his opinion is that the jury's still out on the medical benefits of chromatherapy, the psychological effects are strong. "I thought it would just be a light," he says, "but I'll tell you, I've never taken so many showers in my life. The water looks like it's coming out red, blue, green—it's beautiful and relaxing, which is therapy enough. We mostly use the shower in the dark, and we've had some of our friends come over to try it or take pictures of it."

Chromatherapy may herald a general trend for bolder use of color throughout the bath. A European maker of fixtures and fittings, has brought out a highly colorful bath furnishings line. These cube-shaped cabinets and coordinating faucets come in yellow-orange for an energizing environment and green-blue for a serene one. The cabinets are made of a plastic that glows without the aid of electricity. Even a linens manufacturer is claiming that its technicolor towels have chromatherapeutic effects—and if the psychology is that easy, maybe we've been getting color therapy for longer than we ever knew.

ABOVE: Using LED technology, this basin senses water temperature and controls color.

OPPOSITE TOP: The acrylic in these storage units makes their edges appear to be lit from within.

OPPOSITE MIDDLE: Thanks to fiberoptics, 270 spray channels in this showerhead look like they're shooting colored water.

OPPOSITE: As seen in this very large soaking tub, blue is the color of calm in chromatherapy.

Color jolts the faucet. The single-lever design comes in vivid orange, blue and green (shown).

DECODING COLOR

According to the basic principles of chromatherapy, the colors of the spectrum are believed to have specific healing effects on the human body. Here's a quick summary of their properties:

RED pumps in power and energy, revving up the metabolism. It's used for muscle therapy, sinus congestion and sexual problems; it's also beneficial for the liver.

ORANGE is a general body and system stimulant, strengthening the organs, uplifting one's mood and increasing appetite. It is also thought to help bones absorb calcium.

YELLOW fosters a bright outlook and increases creative and mental clarity, so it's seen as ideal for treating depression. It's also said to have detoxifying and cell-repair effects.

GREEN brings about natural balance, both emotionally and in the nervous system, and so is very healing. It's a stress-reliever nonpareil.

BLUE soothes, plain and simple, though overuse can cause a depressed feeling. It calms inflammation and spasms; and fights infection.

INDIGO works similarly to blue. Rather than include a separate color for indigo, some chromatherapy systems forgo it and add white light to the mix.

VIOLET, with its blend of soothing blue tones and stimulating reds, has a wide range of health applications—including maintaining the immune system at high efficiency; regulating the digestive system; calming feelings of anger; and detoxifying the body.

Zen Palette

BELOW: A bamboo ladder echoes the Asian theme. The owner found it at an antiques shop and decided it was a better spot for towels and washcloths than the heavy rod the builder had chosen.

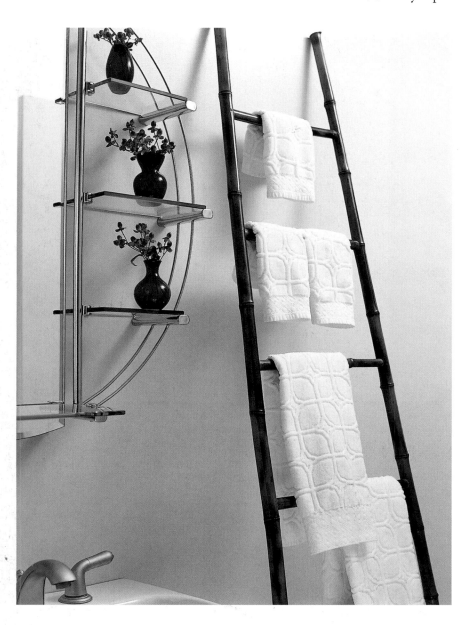

SERENITY WAS THE GUIDING concept behind a to-the-studs remodel of the 6x9-foot bath in this 1920s home in Bethesda, Maryland. Not being a master bath, the room called for no lavish, spa-style fixtures. Furthermore, a dramatic treatment fit for a powder room would have been visually overwhelming for daily use. The homeowners asked Cindy McClure, senior designer at Art Design Build in Bethesda, to create an earth-toned style of Zen-like calm.

The old bath had a 1950s-style pink motif, according to one of the homeowners, Ariella Lerman. The design team gutted the space and, without changing the footprint, transformed it into a neutral, peaceful setting.

Perhaps the most noticeable elements are the 12x12-inch slate tiles on the floor and tub surround. A single batch of slate in a beige color family provided McClure with a wealth of tones to work with.

Bisque-painted walls and porcelain fixtures with sleek curves make modern design statements. "We wanted clean-lined fixtures with a sense of lightness to make the room serene," Ariella says. "Also, we wanted the taupe and cream colors to make it a bit like being in nature, a mood that I find very relaxing."

The chrome-framed mirror with glass shelves deliberately upstages the modest lines and colors. Because so much of the room is linear, the elliptical element takes on even greater drama. The roughness of the bronze Shinto-style sconce and brushed-chrome fittings contrast with the creaminess of the porcelain and the sleek mirror. And then there is the hewn touch of the slate. Other textures in earth tones fill in to add even more tactile richness—perfect for relaxation.

PRECEDING PAGE: This bathroom certainly has more design elements than just the window treatment, but take the drapes away and the mood completely changes. Such accents can be ideal in small spaces, giving the room heaps of personality yet yielding when the homeowner decides to change the look.

RIGHT: When the rest of the room is almost all straight lines, a big ellipse is rather dramatic. Witness this chrome-framed oval mirror with glass shelves.

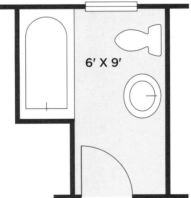

ABOVE: Because of the routine fixture placement in this 6x9-foot space, the designer's magic was mostly limited to aesthetic touches.

FRIVOLOUS TOUCHES

LIGHTEN UP LIFE with a touch of frivolity—even in the bath. These tips will show how a little whimsy can improve even the smallest spaces on the most modest budgets.

STENCIL a school of fish along the wall behind the tub.

DRAPE some fishnet on the wall and embellish it with seashells and starfish.

DRY OFF with oversize brightly striped bath towels.

DECORATE with colorful plastic sand-castle molds.

SEW A BORDER of buttons on a plain shower curtain and use button-style hooks to hang it.

UPHOLSTER a bath chair with a colorful chenille beach towel.

PAINT THE OUTSIDE of a vintage claw-foot tub in a vivid color or festive pattern. (Yes, they can be painted.)

GO HAWAIIAN with a border of hula dancers and paper leis draped over a medicine cabinet.

MOUNT A FRIEZE of paper-doll bathing beauties.

CREATE A TROPICAL OASIS with bamboo patterned textiles and island-themed accessories.

PERCH A HOT-PINK flamingo on the tub for a chuckle.

KEEP FIXTURES and backgrounds neutral and play with colorful,

seasonal accessories: a frog soap dish throughout the spring, bright poppy towels in summer, leaf printed shower curtain for fall and hanging crystal prisms in the wintertime.

USE AN OLD DRAWER as a shelf or shadow box. Line it with an interesting paper or funky fabric, and then use it to display perfume bottles, seashells or old apothecary jars.

BRIGHTEN A BLAND WALL with a border printed with a tropical scene.

THROW DOWN a scatter rug shaped like a rubber ducky.

INSTALL a colorful mosaic tile "rug" on a bathroom floor.

SPICE THINGS UP a bit by changing the color of your sink with specially formulated paint.

USE ANIMAL-SHAPED hooks to hang towels and robes.

MAKE A SHOWER CURTAIN from supergraphic 1970s-style Scandinavian sheets.

INDULGE in inexpensive, but vibrantly colored plastic wastepaper baskets, tissue holders, cups and holders.

STRIPE and tent the walls of the bathroom to resemble a beach cabana.

FRAME a child's robe or apron to adorn a bathroom or kitchen wall.

DRESS UP wall sconces or an overhead light with bright glass beads, hearts or seasonal ornaments.

PAINT A BRICK WALL and stencil it with great big sunflowers or poppies.

STAMP A BARE WALL with rubber duckies, flying fish or bright green frogs.

WALLPAPER with frolicsome prints such as colorful teapots, pink flamingos or retro patterns.

BORDER your walls with nostalgic images of bathing beauties.

TOP: Teapot-patterned wallpaper adds a spark of fun to the room.

ABOVE: Mosaics in shades of bright, aquatic colors provide a cheery face-lift.

LEFT: Capture a contemporary look with this wall mirror. The glass shelves on the 33-inch unit are an ideal spot for toiletries.

22 WAYS TO... UPGRADE YOUR BATH ON A BUDGET

THE SIMPLEST ALTERATIONS CAN ADD NEW LIFE and appeal to a bath without the hassle of a major remodel. Paint, wallpaper, trims, tiles, updated accessories and other accents can provide instant upgrades for dated spaces.

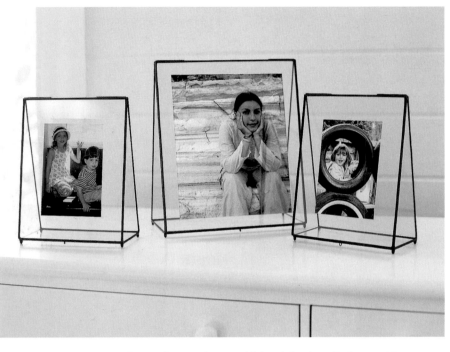

ABOVE: Move some framed pictures into the bath for a sophisticated but friendly touch. Changing the photos from time to time is an inexpensive way to revitalize the space.

RIGHT: Conceal the flaws in a less-than-perfect floor—or just go for a change of scenery—with a bold but pocketbook-friendly paint treatment. Just tape off a simple pattern and choose the colors.

• Conceal blemished walls by tacking up beadboard paneling. Top with a shelf to hold toiletries.
• Paint a faux-marble finish on a vanity. Remember to seal it against water.
• Replace limp curtains with a set of crisp plantation shutters.
• Transform a clawfoot tub by painting a vibrant color on its exterior. Add towels and accessories to match.
• Revitalize a rusted tub with a specially fitted acrylic cover.
• Revive a vanity by removing the lower doors. Paint it inside and out. Store towels in wicker baskets displayed on the shelves.
• Stamp painted walls with charming floral or funky figurative designs.
• If an old linoleum floor is still intact, jazz it up with paint. (Be sure the paint will adhere and stand up to moisture.) Be creative with designs on alternating tiles, and paint trompe l'oeil "mats" in front of the tub and by the doorway.
• Change shower curtains every season, and hang them with whimsical or fancy hooks. In the fall, for example, glue silk leaves on grosgrain ribbons to make shower-curtain ties.
• Incorporate shards of broken ceramic tiles into a mosaic top for a bathroom vanity or small table. Affix pieces in a decorative pattern to a bed of tile adhesive. Fill in with grout.
• Forage for funky metal furniture. Old medical cabinets or office pieces can be left "as is" or painted. They make wonderful storage places for towels and toiletries.
• Install a pair of fun sconces on either side of the mirror over the sink.
• Personalize the walls with easily removable peel-and-stick art images.

LEFT: Pretty as well as practical, towels in au courant colors can give a sparkling new personality to the bath.

BELOW: It's all in the accessories. Even something as simple as adding a bud vase (or two) in a happy hue can boost a bathroom.

• Purchase shower curtains and floor mats that coordinate—or contrast—with the existing floor tiles.

• Sew a skirt for a pedestal sink and trim the window or shower curtains with leftover lengths of fabric.

• Add artsy touches like painted plates, framed architectural prints or a series of black-and-white photos to the walls.

• Wallpaper with one of the most current designs. Some styles are even available that mimic the look of tile.

• Stick with basic white for walls and fixtures, but paint the ceiling a surprising color like hot pink or sky-blue.

• Update a vinyl floor with a painted finish. (Use several coats of latex paint.) Embellish with a stamped design and cover with polyurethane.

• Apply vinyl appliqués to existing tiles.

• Introduce plants that thrive on moisture into the room for a tropical feel.

• Decorate roller shades with patterns to complement the decor of the room.

About Face-lift

OF ALL THE CHANGES MADE in this second-floor bathroom, none had more impact than the decision to move the plumbing fittings in the tub/shower from one end to the other. This opened the room up to additional sunlight, which in turn made the space feel larger.

Brenda and Charles Gordon had lived in their Tudor-style cottage near downtown Toronto, Canada, for more than a dozen years before deciding to get to work on their second-floor bathroom. They had to—it was, in effect, their only bathroom—because the other one was in the unused maid's quarters in the basement.

Brenda wanted the new bath to be a showplace, but she thought that goal would mean encroaching on a nearby staircase or absorbing part of the adjacent master bedroom. Clearly, she needed design help to make the most of a room whose dimensions barely exceeded 7x8 feet—a room that had not been altered since the 1970s.

The Gordons found design ideas in magazines, just like any prospective remodeling customer, but they found something else, too. "I read an article on kitchen and bathroom renovations in a style magazine," Brenda recalls. "It had pictures of bathrooms Erica Westeroth designed. I got in touch with her, and she came up with a design that was absolutely right for us."

Working within the room's existing shell, Westeroth, of XTC Design in Toronto, oversaw the removal of the old plumbing fixtures and worked with the Gordons to select replacements. The big change occurred with the design of the combination tub/shower. Instead of reinstalling a showerhead in the wall closer to the windows, Westeroth reversed its position, built a partition wall that was half tile and half glass, and designed a set of frameless glass doors for the shower. The glass enclosure does two things: It brings ambient light into the shower, and it opens up the room visually, cutting down the cramped factor as much as possible.

To upgrade the room, the Gordons splurged on 12x12-inch Spanish marble for walls, countertops and flooring—polished on all but the floor where slip-resistant tiles are a safer option.

LEFT: A custom vanity with honey-finished maple doors occupies one side of this all-purpose bath. An oval mirror, mounted on a mirrored wall, echoes a 21x12-inch oval sink that fits neatly into a countertop that measures barely 18 inches deep. Adding to the room's elegant look are stainless steel sink fittings and brushed-nickel cabinet knobs.

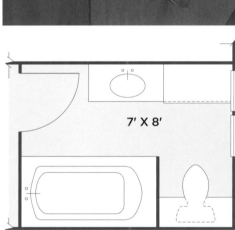

7' X 8'

MAKING ROOM

Maximizing a fairly limited space was the goal of designer Erica Westeroth and her clients. Together they agreed to:

COLLAPSE THE DEPTH of the vanity to make room for a more spacious tub-shower combination unit.

PLACE A STORAGE CABINET BESIDE THE VANITY that's tall enough to hold towels and linens without blocking the windows.

MOUNT AN ADDITIONAL STORAGE CABINET on the wall behind the toilet for anything that can't fit in the other two cabinets.

CHOOSE A BEIGE-AND-WHITE COLOR SCHEME to keep the room from feeling crowded. Cabinet fronts were stained to pick up the rust-toned veining in the marble.

REPLACE THE TALL, UGLY RADIATOR with a baseboard model and supplement that with electric radiant heating under the floor.

ABOVE LEFT: The home's diamond-shaped leaded-glass windows were repaired, and an eyesore radiator that stood under them was removed. In its place is a more understated baseboard unit. Marble floor tiles were set on the diagonal to visually stretch the space.

TOP: An undersink drawer holds bath essentials. It has two separate bins with open space in between to allow for the drainpipe.

ABOVE: Fixture placements remain the same in the new bath, and the dimensions are unchanged, too. To make room for the wider tub/shower, the designer shrank the depth of the vanity.

OPPOSITE: Sunlight now floods the bath. There are glass doors on the tub-shower and a glass half-wall on the toilet partition.

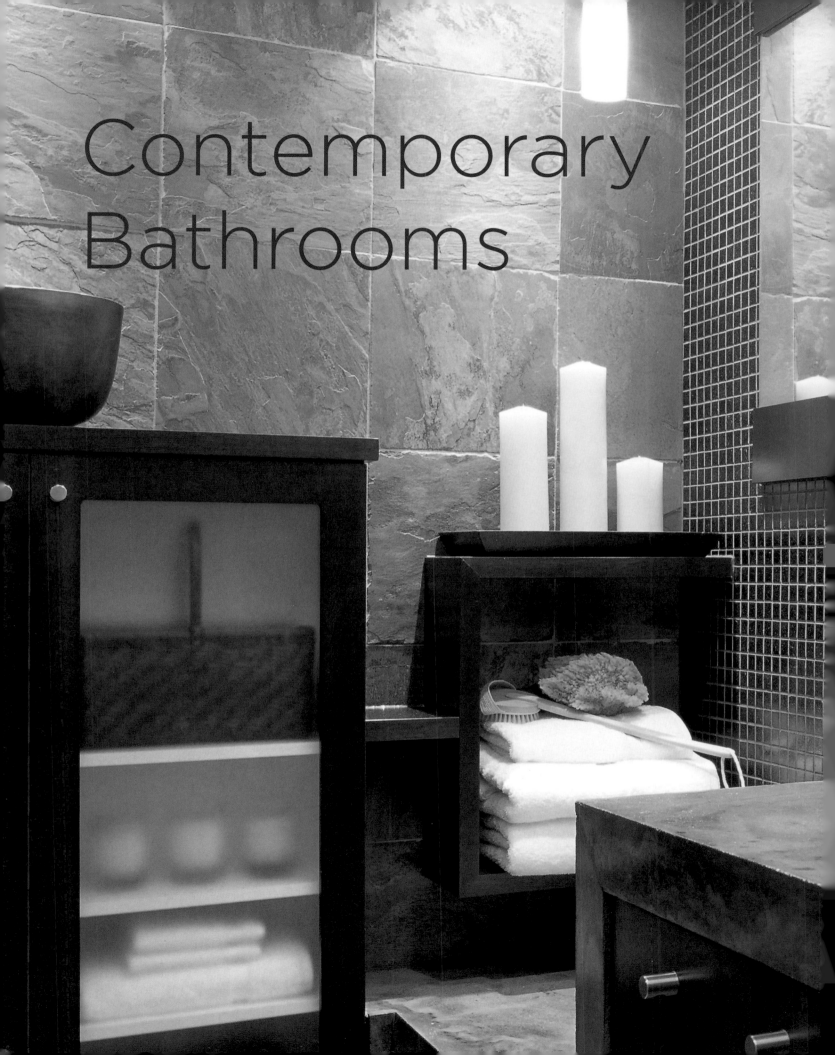

Contemporary
Bathrooms

Functional Fun

UNIQUE, WHIMSICAL AND MODERN are the three factors Donna and Jim Zocco emphasized in this bathroom, in addition to overcoming a host of practical shortcomings in their old space. The modern part rubbed against the style of the couple's 1980s brick Colonial in Modlothian, Virginia, but this turned out to be no problem. Designer David Raber, of Classic Kitchens of Virginia in Richmond, feels that sometimes a room remodel is not about maintaining stylistic continuity with the rest of the home. So he created a complete departure, a highly personalized, individual space that's markedly distinct from the decor found anywhere else in the house.

As for those practical shortcomings, the original bath was, in a word, horrendous. The toilet was in plain view of the bathroom door, the shower was dark and small, storage space was nearly nonexistent, and a brown whirlpool tub invaded the center of the room.

To enlarge the space, Raber appropriated 3½ feet from the end of the master bedroom, a move that also improved the proportions of the long, narrow bedroom. Once that was done, it was time for the fun to begin.

The designer gives Donna credit for picking the wall color, and he says her idea was a good one. Indeed, the purple walls are a natural fit with the tiles of multi-colored Indian slate that cover the floor and the shower enclosure. The twin sinks, vanity top and tub surround were fabricated from four colors of solid surfacing, including a distinctive lavender shade. The bone color of the sinks and tub surround matches the almond tub and toilet. Custom maple cabinets find a close match in the wood-grain laminate that curves around the drum-like sink bases.

The simple recessed panels of the cabinets contrast with the traditional raised-panel doors found throughout the house—even on the his-and-her closets that are situated at one end of the bath. This contrast continues the bathroom's theme of a modern statement juxtaposed against a traditional backdrop.

The ample whirlpool tub is now tucked into a corner, which means it is no longer an obstruction. Three nearly invisible floating frames are set into the mirrored wall behind the tub. These frames, one of Raber's favorite details, can serve as shelves for bathing products or candles. A simple showerhead is the only fitting in the spacious, well-lighted shower with a built-in bench. This spare arrangement keeps the focus on the size

RIGHT: The spacious plan accommodates several large storage units; the doors on the right side of the room lead to dressing rooms and closets.

and rich stone surfaces of the enclosure. A wall-mounted electric towel warmer is convenient to both shower and tub.

Finally, the toilet—formerly front and center—is now tucked discreetly into a recess next to the shower. Instead of being exposed, a handsome maple storage cabinet now shields the toilet from the entrance to the bathroom.

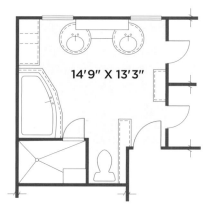

14'9" X 13'3"

GOOD IDEAS

GET PERSONAL: Rooms can represent a homeowner's sensibilities, even if that means departing from the look of the rest of the house. For example, a staid Colonial is home to this zingy master bath. Break the rules smartly, and the results can be magic.
OUTSIDE INFLUENCES: Be open to ideas. The inspiration for the distinctive rounded sink bases in the Zocco bath came from an advertisement for solid surfacing that Donna spotted in a magazine.
GET HELP: Those overwhelmed with too many choices of fixtures and fittings should ask a designer to narrow the possibilities and present a more limited, educated selection.

RIGHT: A half-wall shields the toilet from direct view and provides shelving for storage of toiletries and linens.

CONTEMPORARY

ABOVE: Incorporating four different hues of solid surfacing, the cylindrical vanity arranges forms and colors in a creative way. Twin integral sinks maintain the clean lines of the cabinet.

ABOVE: The glass panels on the front of this storage cabinet help reflect daylight into the bathroom. Their translucent finish lets the colors and shapes of the contents show and become part of the decor.

OPPOSITE ABOVE: A generous stack of shallow drawers with a cabinet on top lets the homeowners organize and store various-size items efficiently.

OPPOSITE BELOW: An adjustable pole storage system, outfitted with a swiveling makeup mirror and trays, helps keep the counter clutter-free.

LIGHTING

When coordinating bathroom lighting, combine fashion with function to make sure your fixtures supply an ample amount of light. Check with professionals at lighting stores to get the broadest range of styles and knowledge.

SHOWER POWER: Lighting in the shower stall should be bright enough to help prevent falls, and it should make shaving and shampooing easier. Choose light fixtures that are designed and rated especially for use in wet areas.

TUB TIP: Tubs, like showers, need good general light. A good recessed fixture can perform this function nicely. To avoid irritating glare, focus the beam towards the outside edge of the bathtub.

NIGHT BRIGHT: Create a striking night light by illuminating the toekick space below vanities and cabinets with a linear lighting system.

GET GLOWING: For a purely aesthetic touch, add cove lighting. These hidden, indirect light sources add a soft, warm glow by bouncing light off walls or the ceiling.

MIRROR, MIRROR: Good mirror lighting, like that from warm vertical fluorescent wall sconces, provides the even illumination necessary to get rid of dark face shadows.

VANITY FARE: A halogen light above the vanity provides cross-illumination when used in conjunction with wall sconces.

TABLE TOPPER: Table lamps add a personal element to a bathroom. To avoid electrocution, always keep them away from water sources.

BATHROOM STORAGE

MANY A SPOUSE HAS HAD TO CALM a frazzled partner who just rifled through disarrayed drawers and chaotic cabinets and still did not find that new toothbrush. Poor organization costs time and definitely frays tempers. When planning a storage scheme, making lists of every item in the bathroom definitely helps. Then divide the lists into categories of use and size, to see how much and what kind of storage the room will need. Here are three smart strategies on how to stash in the bath.

1. UNDER THE COUNTER

CLOCKWISE FROM ABOVE:
The unusual swinging drawer that's built into the chrome frame of this console basin has a removable plastic interior for easy cleaning.

The undercounter storage features in this multi-featured stainless steel unit include a built-in towel rack, integral toilet paper holder and a side cabinet with adjustable shelves.

Dropping a short stack of three Wenge-wood drawers between two wall-hung lavs creates a handy open surface, some space between sink users and enclosed, compartmentalized storage.

A simple shelf with radius-front drawer provides basic undercounter storage in the elegant console table.

This cleverly contoured drawer interior rescues dead space that's typically lost to the bottom of the wash basin.

2. ON THE WALL

CLOCKWISE FROM ABOVE LEFT:
Flanked by slatted cherry ladders, this bathroom mirror anchors a flexible, modern storage system.

To accommodate the specialized plumbing of the laminar flow faucet (the little eye near the bottom), this mirrored cabinet has shelves that slide out to the side.

Crafted of beech wood, the offset door of this medicine cabinet conceals most of its contents; then again, shelves extend past the edge of the mirror, making display space for the classiest toiletries.

Hung beyond the reach of curious kids, the upward-opening doors of this 27-inch-wide x 35-inch-tall x 8-inch-deep cabinet allow for installation in narrow confines.

Mounted on the wall with brackets, the mirror spins around to reveal two storage compartments. The bottoms of the bins are removable for cleaning. The unit measures 9 inches wide x 24 inches tall x 5½ inches deep.

3. STAND ALONE

CLOCKWISE FROM ABOVE LEFT: Set on easy-rolling casters, this 32-inch-tall x 13-inch-wide x 14-inch-deep chrome taboret features two melamine-lined drawers and a compartment with a removable shelf.

These slender cabinets and shelves (often called "totem" units) are well suited for tight bathroom spaces—they make the most of vertical space.

With ribbed-glass door insert, these two towel lockers can comfortably straddle contemporary and traditional decors.

The mobile storage cart comes with side and front panels in wenge, birch, maple or white wood finishes. Door and drawer pulls are made of aluminum and are available either square or rounded.

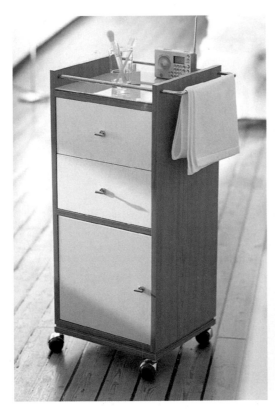

17 WAYS TO...
STRETCH STORAGE

THINK THE BATHROOM STORAGE SPACE HAS BEEN MAXED OUT?
Don't despair! Savvy planners can steal space from unexpected sources. Find wasted space under cabinets, in drawers, behind toekicks or on walls, and add drawer inserts, lazy Susans and slide-out shelves. Read on for storage-stretching tips.

• Transform a wine rack into a storage unit for rolled-up towels.
• Put ceramic knobs on the back of a door for hanging robes.
• Attach a Peg-Board to the wall to hold laundry bags or baskets.
• Tilt a stylized ladder against a wall to hang towels.
• Store extra towels on translucent plastic shelves above the doorway.
• Include a hamper stool for both a comfy seat and a place for storage.
• Tuck reading material into a wall-mounted magazine rack.
• Mount a hair dryer unit onto the wall near your mirror—just like hotels do.
• Turn storage into a decorative feature with a pocketed plastic shower curtain. Tuck shampoo bottles, tub toys and extra soap into the pockets.
• Wrap wire around simple glass vases and hang them on nails in the wall. Store makeup brushes, lipsticks, eyeliners and mascara wands in them.

ABOVE LEFT: Adding a teak ladder provides decorative vertical storage for towels and magazines.

ABOVE: Roll-out wire baskets keep towels and other bathroom essentials neatly tucked away yet easily accessible.

LEFT: A wicker basket offers an attractive spot to conceal facial tissue and toilet paper.

• Add a tilt-out bin under a vanity for laundry or a small hamper.
• Take advantage of the deep space in under-sink cabinets with lazy Susans.
• Build a narrow side cabinet to hide the toilet area and provide storage.
• Replace an outdated medicine cabinet with one that has open shelves, pegs or cubbies on either side.
• Store extra bottles of shampoo and conditioner on door-mounted shelf units inside cabinets.
• Tuck towels out of sight in a vanity on sliding racks.
• Hang a shelf next to the tub for bubble bath and shampoos.

Japan-tastic

STYLISTIC TASTE CAN LAST A LIFETIME. "When I was in the Navy in 1954," this homeowner says, "my wife and I set up housekeeping in Kamakura, Japan, and fell in love with Japanese style—its cedar ceilings and the beauty of its woodworking." After returning stateside, the couple incorporated Japanese elements into their own new home.

Fast-forward four decades. Fortunate enough to reach their early 70s still fit and flexible, both husband and wife knew physical limitations could loom in the future. So when they decided to add a master bath, their requirements were clear: They needed a space that would remain fully accessible throughout their senior years and maintain the pleasing Japanese aesthetic of the home. Accordingly, they faced two choices: Either sell their beloved house and "move to someplace simpler," or take on the remodeling that would let them stay put indefinitely. The decision required little thought, as the husband admits, "I can't get my wife out of her garden."

With help from designer Beverly Staal, the couple extended the house by about 8 feet to create space for the new bath off the master bedroom. The entry doorway and the opening leading to the shower measure an oversize 43 and 42 inches wide, respectively, giving access to wheelchair users if necessary. Staal left the shower door out, eliminating both a space-breaker and a potential obstacle. Only a curtain and a panel of patterned glass define the open shower area. A partition separates this area from the toilet, but the divider can go in the future to provide more maneuvering room.

Material selection respects the Asian ambience of the home. Satin-finish ceramic tiles in neutral tones cover the floor and walls. Lengths of cedar for the ceiling were stained to match ceilings elsewhere in the house. Constructed of vertical-grain fir, the vanity and storage cabinet echo the simple lines of Japanese woodwork. Sunk halfway into the granite top of the vanity is a glass-bowl sink, which the owners consider "a lovely sculptural piece that makes something beautiful out of a tool for daily living." (The shape of the sink repeats the oval of the mirror above it. The homeowners requested these ovals to soften the angular lines of the room.)

A sliding shoji-style screen serves as the room's door, its translucent-fiberglass panels much more durable than rice paper. Near the foot of the tub, another screen closes the bath from the bedroom. The full-height cabinet has more sliding panels in the center, and three translucent-glass panes in that cabinet conceal a medicine chest.

PRECEDING PAGES: Instead of traditional rice paper, these shoji-style screens are made of translucent fiberglass, which holds up better in a damp environment.

ABOVE: Wide passageways, the lack of doorsills and ample central open space combine to make this master bathroom suite both comfortable and accommodating.

The room owes much of its sense of spaciousness to large windows. "The site is completely private, like living in a tree house," says the husband. What's more, in spring, the skylight frames a view of blossoming plum and dogwood trees.

Blending beauty and accessibility, this space shows wise planning and a timeless appeal. As long as the homeowners live here, the design will serve them well.

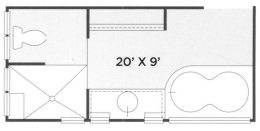

ABOVE: Using sliding shoji-style screens as partitions in the room eliminates space-consuming door-swing areas.

LEFT: The tub features a sloped back support, which enhances comfort and reduces the amount of water needed to fill the tub.

BELOW: Small accent tiles of earthy tumbled stone interspersed with mirrored squares add visual interest to the shower walls and beyond.

GOOD IDEAS

LOOK AHEAD: The homeowners admit it didn't occur to them to plan for accessibility when they designed their home in the 1960s. Many years later, they're fit and healthy, but even so, they are delighted to have such easy, flowing access in their new bath, unimpeded by narrow doorways or raised sills.

TILE STYLE: On walls and most of the floor, 12-inch satin-finish ceramic tile in a neutral color creates a tranquil backdrop. A 6-inch version of the same tile lines the windowsills, and the shower floor is covered with 3-inch tiles for maximum traction. The homeowners are enthusiastic about their radiant-heating system, which cycles on and off to warm the floor tiles to a constant 71°F.

JET SET: The jetted bathtub was chosen with care. "We hadn't been into tubbing for 40 years," the husband says, but the couple finds the massage tub "more useful and comfortable than we'd thought."

Lights, More Lights, Action

EVERYONE FORGOT ABOUT GOOD LIGHTING all over North America at some point during the 20th century. Otherwise, so many bathrooms (and kitchens, for that matter) wouldn't be in such dire need of brightening. This master bathroom, for example, has four interior walls and absolutely no possibility of a window. Toronto condominium owners Jay Junnila and Peter DeVries turned to Erica Westeroth, of XTC Design, also in Toronto, to solve this lighting conundrum and convert the uninspired bath into a dramatic and contemporary space.

"We wanted the same clean, modern lines as in the rest of the apartment," says Jay. "But those rooms were light and airy. Then we hit on the idea of a juxtaposition: The bath could be a modern but warm, cave-like room in dark colors with soft lighting."

First, the floor plan needed an overhaul. Westeroth totally revamped the layout by removing a corner tub, enclosing the shower in glass, and making more counter space and storage. In the process, she made the room feel much more open. She had to do things this way, as the walls couldn't be repositioned, according to condominium bylaws.

Eliminating the tub created a lot more space, and the glass shower enclosure means the eye doesn't meet obstacles as it scans around the room. The lines of the shower, mirror and waterfall countertop all create squares and rectangles, forging a serenity with an Asian flavor. Furthermore, straight lines dominate, and the room is free of awkward angles that would introduce visual tension.

Several key added elements give the room its character. Westeroth designed a showstopping vanity and storage bench with a polished concrete top that steps down, making an abstract reference to falling water. cherry wood base cabinets run the length of the room.

The floor plan and geometry set a soothing stage, and lively, original material choices create a rich, impressive mood. Rough limestone tiles in deep gold boldly announce their grain on the floor and walls. Black glass tiles on the vanity wall form a dramatic foil for the mirror. Concrete on the counter was an inspired idea from the designer, Jay says: "It's unexpected to find the smooth, cool touch of concrete when you walk in,

PRECEDING PAGES: The concrete countertop has an integrated sink. Installations like this one start with wooden molds that are used only one time. This type of concrete work is a custom shape and size and is usually poured on site.

BELOW: With the glass shelves recessed into a niche, the plane of the wall remains visually intact, keeping the space pure.

OPPOSITE ABOVE: A shower enclosure of anything but glass would create a bulky obstacle in the room and obscure the view of the limestone walls.

especially seen against the limestone. Guests at our parties really notice it."

And of course, there's that lighting scheme. Pot lights tucked in the ceiling cast a glow on the walls, and decorative pendants can illuminate a lot or a little. "I'm big on dimmers," Jay says. "I can adjust them to make the early morning atmosphere more comforting."

At the remodel's end, Peter—who hadn't been heavily involved—was impressed at how well everything came together. "He was skeptical that we could do dark tones that didn't feel oppressive," Jay says, "but now he's very happy with it."

ask the experts

How do you prevent mold and mildew from forming on a bathroom ceiling?

Adequate ventilation is absolutely vital; it's one of the preeminent concerns in a room that's all about cleanliness. That means installing a durable, good-quality fan. Fans should provide about eight to 10 air-exchanges per hour. Maximize their efficiency by placing them near the shower, and vent them to the outdoors. Venting humid air into an attic can cause materials to rot. Fan efficiency is also affected by static pressure, created by obstacles such as grilles, and especially by the length of the ductwork. This efficiency is akin to drinking milk through a straw; the longer the straw, the harder the draw. Seek professional advice to determine what fan strength—in CFM (cubic feet per minute)—is needed in a space.

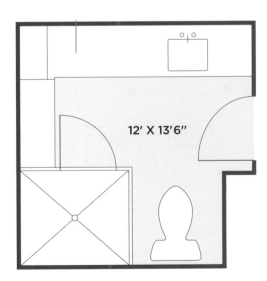

ABOVE: Eliminating a corner tub opened up the room and created a blank slate for the designer, who emphasized the rectangular shape of the space with custom forms and finishes.

WHAT MAKES IT WORK

A mix of textures is the alchemy that gives a room real sensuality—when the eyes read texture, they automatically register how the surface would feel on the skin. This bath employs a surprisingly wide variety of textures in a 12x13½-foot space.

THE ROUGH LIMESTONE tiles have rustic grains, and yet limestone is a soft stone with a slightly buttery look, depending on the light.

THE BLACK GLASS TILES on the sink wall are cold and smooth. They are so small, however, that the grout lines form a large component of the composition. The lines' rough texture actually competes for attention.

THE CHERRY WOOD of the cabinets was sanded very smooth and stained a dark russet brown.

GLASS SHOWER WALLS conjure up the transparent deluge of water.

A WALL NICHE with glass shelves makes a sleeker impression than the medicine cabinet it replaced.

THE GLASS PANEL in the linen-cabinet door isn't clear—it's frosted, a better look for concealing toiletries and other personal items.

CONCRETE POLISHED to smoothness is cool to the touch. The shape of this counter is also pleasingly chunky—that, too, invites touching.

CHERRY WOOD FRAMES only the top and bottom of an almost-wall-length mirror. The sides of the glass are unframed, creating a textural contrast on the piece.

CHROME-FINISH DRAWER pulls and a sink faucet that combines shiny and brushed finishes add a little more playful contrasts.

TWO SOURCES OF LIGHT on dimmers can be adjusted to enhance textural contrasts.

RIGHT: The continuous stretch of counter drops down to form a built-in bench where the concrete meets the wall.

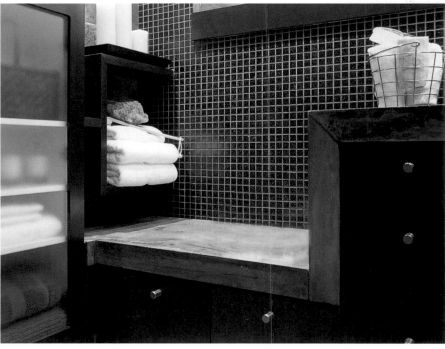

48 WAYS TO...
FRESHEN THE BATHROOM

THOUGH SPRING CLEANING IS A RITUAL for many, freshening things up before that season is another way to ensure that indoor spaces have a clean, cheerful and pleasant ambience throughout the darker and shorter days of autumn and winter.

ABOVE: A crown molding changes the personality of a staid medicine cabinet.

BELOW: Drapes and wallpaper go a long way in establishing a look.

WALLS

• Paint them! Lighten the look to brighten the entire space.
• Camouflage aging or yellowing tile with specially formulated paint, or start all over with a pristine white.
• Get a splash of color. Paint the tub nook in a contrasting shade from that of the rest of the space.
• Hang new pictures. Color-copy favorite prints or use digital travel photos for a quick fix. These methods allow for easy replacement in case of humidity damage.
• Add an interesting border to complement the existing wallpaper or enhance painted surfaces.
• Stencil a montage of water fowl, shells or sea critters on one wall or around a medicine cabinet.
• Indulge in a bit of luxury with a tiled backsplash over the sink.
• Mount glass vases and candleholders to the wall for a romantic feel.

WINDOWS

• Mount a valance over the existing shower curtain using a spring-loaded rod. Repeat the treatment at a window.
• Make a floral or paisley pocket for the rod and tiebacks to update the look of a solid-color shower curtain.
• Sew a border of bright grosgrain ribbon on a favorite shower curtain. (Again, don't forget the matching window treatment.)
• Create a new shower curtain and Roman shade quickly and inexpensively from bedroom sheets.
• Replace limp curtains with faux-bamboo shades or faux-wood blinds. (The humidity in a bathroom can be hard on real bamboo and real wood.)

FLOORS

• Pull up pile carpeting (please!) and scatter a few cheerful chenille rugs.
• Revitalize wooden floors with several coats of marine paint.
• Install new linoleum floor tiles.
• Brighten dingy grout in ceramic-tile floors with white shoe polish.
• Jazz things up with a brightly colored bath mat.

DECORATIVE TOUCHES

• Dress up wooden doorknobs with hand-painted flowers, seashells, anchors or other nautical symbols.
• Add plants for a natural look.
• Change the hardware on cabinets.
• Replace shower curtain hooks with Lucite clips or simple metal rings.
• Have fun with accessories. Corral soaps and sponges in a vintage enamel bucket or, for a more contemporary look, in a metal champagne bucket.
• Indulge in crisp white towels.
• Decoupage a wastebasket and tissue holder with postcards, travel brochures, seed packets or snapshots.
• Tilt a ladder against the wall to hold extra towels, taking advantage of bare vertical space.
• Buy a new toothbrush holder, soap dish and lotion dispenser.
• Tear out a tatty vanity and retrofit a dresser or table to hold the sink.
• Remove cabinet doors, paint or cover the shelves with fabric and display towels and baskets within.
• Cover up rusted or ugly pipes with a simple terry-cloth skirt attached to the sink with hook-and-loop tape.
• Choose new chrome or brass fittings.

- Create towel bars from clear plastic tubes. Fill the plastic tubes with beads, confetti or potpourri. Attach the tubes to wooden mounts.
- Add a glass shelf over the sink to hold extra toiletries or glass votive containers.
- Paint laminate countertops with oil-based semi gloss paint to rejuvenate them without a lot of fuss.
- Give the room a fresh country feel with an antique washstand or porcelain basin and pitcher, perhaps from a yard sale.
- Spray wicker baskets in colors to match curtains and decorate with complementary motifs and patterns.
- Fold and stack towels on a simple, painted step stool.
- Retire an old medicine cabinet and replace it with a large framed mirror.

PRACTICAL POINTERS

- Hang a Shaker peg shelf to display monogrammed linen hand towels.
- Cover switch plates with leftover wallpaper or fabric so that they complement the decor.
- Station a freestanding wrought-iron tissue holder near the toilet.
- Change ornamental accessories with the seasons: Perch bathing beauty statues on shelves in summer, ceramic fruit in fall, crystal perfume bottles in winter and flowers in spring.
- Tuck an étagère in a corner to hold accessories and necessities.
- Display hand towels or jewelry on an iron tabletop towel stand.
- Plug in night-lights—they are both attractive and practical.

- Line wicker hampers with fabric for laundry or storage.
- Sort dirty clothes stylishly with individual, stenciled hampers for whites, darks and fragile laundry.
- Get back to basics with a simple wooden rack to hold robes.

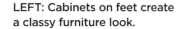

LEFT: Cabinets on feet create a classy furniture look.

BELOW: Over-the-door hooks are a quick, stylish addition.

BELOW FAR LEFT AND LEFT: Color mesh baskets and open wire racks with colorful towels are an easy way to add both organization and vibrance.

BOTTOM: A sink on a washstand gives a sort of country feel.

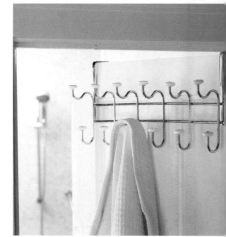

Young at Heart

ALEX ATWELL LUCKED OUT when parents Linda and Jamie bought a five-bedroom hilltop home in La Jolla, California. The entire second floor became a suite for the boy, age 2 at the time. His huge bedroom flows into a carpeted playroom. The bath originally had a tub and an "ugly, separate shower," Linda says. Its 14-foot ceiling, 7x17-foot perimeter and less-than-3-foot user gave Alex's parents as many challenges as opportunities.

For advice on dealing with the bath—and other areas of the 1980s-era house—the Atwells turned to their longtime decorator, Janice Elder, of Home Sweet Home in Moorestown, New Jersey. A professional decorator, Elder also happens to be Linda's mother. She suggested the bath's new layout, and then Heather Moe, of South Pacific Kitchen & Construction in La Jolla, came on board to design plumbing, cabinets and all the aesthetic details.

The idea was to make this bath, like the rest of the upstairs suite, a setting Alex would feel comfortable in as he grew and matured, and one that would also welcome a sibling, should the Atwells decide to expand their family. Thus, though there are touches of whimsy, specifically in the tile design, nothing is babyish about the bath decor.

The design team worked within the room's original walls. As with the previous incarnation doors lead to the bedroom and a walk-in closet. Pre-existing clerestory windows flood the room with daylight. What the team added were tall partitions between the toilet, secondary sink and tub/shower, and between the tub/shower and the vanity. A pocket door they installed creates a privacy barrier between the bathing/sanitary and dressing/grooming areas.

The only concession to child-size needs is the granite-top vanity, which is just under 30 inches high. The raised rectangular sink is big enough to bathe a baby—should Alex ever have a sibling with whom to share the space. The flooring is gray pebbles anchored to foot-square mesh. Once the mesh was in place, off-white grout was poured on and allowed to set overnight. The result is a textured floor that anchors the space and also provides a slip-proof surface—a welcome feature in a bath for kids.

Because her child's bath was upstairs, somewhat removed from the heart of the house, Linda Atwell wanted to make sure it contained adequate storage for all cleaning, bathing and grooming needs, whether it would be used by one, two or more children. So Moe placed cherry

PRECEDING PAGES: At 30 inches high, the vanity is designed for children. It has a long counter that could be used as a changing table, should the Atwells have another baby, and the oversize, raised sink is scaled for baby bathing.

BELOW: The tiltable sink faucet handle—hot to the left, cold to the right—was picked because the Atwells knew it would bring a smile to anyone who used it.

cabinets, generous enough for bathroom essentials, on two opposing walls. The vanity has two open shelves for fresh towels, along with drawers and closed cupboards for soaps and grooming products.

Directly opposite the tub/shower is a cabinet with three doors, plus a series of niches for toys, more towels and anything worthy of display. "I envision putting delightful things there that Alex would enjoy," says Linda. "I haven't found the perfect objects yet." Maybe Alex (or a sibling or two) will come up with a few ideas so she doesn't have to.

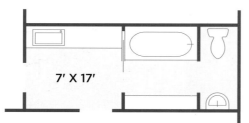

7' X 17'

ABOVE: The proportions didn't change, but the elements were rearranged. Now a grooming area is at one end and a bathing and sanitary area at the other. A pocket door creates the possibility of privacy.

TILE TALE

The Atwells chose glass tile for the tub deck and shower stall and as trim around the vanity. Linda says she was careful to create a pattern that was sophisticated as well as whimsical: "Actually, I didn't want any kind of pattern at all. The tiles came in one-foot squares. We kept turning them to create a random arrangement." The tile color scheme—gray-blue and gray-green—is a far cry from what one might expect in a child's bath and pivotal to this bathroom suite's overall appeal. Add in the floor of grouted beach pebbles, and the end result is a bath that would be right for a child of any age and any gender. This, of course, is the whole point of the plan.

ABOVE: Adjustable and handheld showerheads rule in children's baths. Handhelds make the process easier on parents, and kids get a kick out of that warm, gentle spray. Adjustables can save energy by bringing the water source closer to the bather, thereby reducing in-transit temperature loss.

ARTY IDEAS

PAINT A SMALL BATHROOM soft blue and hang a vibrant sea-life shower curtain.

CHOOSE WALLPAPER with a stylized fish design for a retro bathroom conversion.

STORE HAND TOWELS in a beach bag.

PAINT A BATHROOM the color of the water in a Virgin Islands inlet and add a souvenir seashell as a soap dish to capture memories of a perfect day in the sun.

DECOUPAGE A WALL with photocopied pictures of marine life. Attach lengths of boat rope to the wall to hold towels and hang a sailboat model on the wall.

FRAME OLD BATHING SUIT ADS or vintage beach scenes for a powder room.

CUT A WAVE PATTERN from a length of white corrugated paper and use it as a window border or picture frame.

TRIM TOWELS WITH RIBBONS decorated with woven images of shells, whales, fish or even frogs.

EMBELLISH THE FRAME of a medicine cabinet mirror with shells.

CREATE A MOSAIC of shell fragments and sea glass for the floor or wall.

ADD A VIBRANT CORAL ACCENT to a spare white bathroom.

ABOVE: Art lovers may see the spirit of Piet Mondrian in the tiles framing the vanity, tub deck and shower stall, but kids will more likely see a playful design that will still be cool when they're a little older.

Compact Makeup

OPPOSITE: This room is meant to convey luxury at first blush, which it does with a combination of the console, spacious shower and mirror with built-in wall sconces.

GLORIOUS LUXURY was this remodel's raison d'etre. Owner Mike Ang wanted his master bath to sing with luxury. "I wanted the bathroom to feel inviting—pampering—a space you enjoy being in." To accomplish that, he needed a professional, as the space was only 46 square feet.

The specialist he brought in was interior designer Sally Power, of San Francisco, who had remodeled the kitchen in Mike's San Francisco condominium. Many times, the designer leads a remodeling job, and the client nods approvingly. In this case, Mike had the vision that this small bathroom should be special, showy and luxurious.

Right off the bat, though, true luxury seemed unlikely, as Power had no way of expanding the space. After some hand wringing, the client/designer team came up with a simple solution: Remove the existing bathtub. This gave Power the room to create the show-stopping shower Mike coveted; everything else rested on materials, fittings and designer sleight-of-hand.

With the layout in place, the design took shape around the first fixture they chose, an Italian console sink made of beech wood, granite, glass and chrome. Mike brought in a double showerhead (to which they added an adjustable hand-shower) and an imported toilet with a hygienic seat with cleansing water jets. Power tied the space together with Calacata Oro marble tile on the walls, trimmed with a wide band of mosaic tile and grounded with porcelain Quarzo Nero floor tiles. Of all the tile, the big draw is the mosaic wall trim. "Everyone who visits the bath remarks on it," Mike says.

To visually expand the tiny room, Power mirrored the wall above the vanity. Although this touch created the illusion of space, it posed a storage problem, because

BELOW: A wide band of mosaic tile circumnavigates nearly the entire space—yet another classy flourish.

it eliminated room for a medicine cabinet. Ever resourceful, Power realized she could recess a narrow, 7-inch-deep cabinet into the opposite wall. The unit she created has a frosted-glass door trimmed in ash. The wood frame has been custom finished to match the vanity.

As final touches, Power painted the walls and ceilings of the room with silver paint for further space-extending reflection and richness. She also added a marble Buddha to the corner seat in the shower as a not-too-overt reference to Mike's Asian heritage.

Designer and client couldn't be more pleased. "The feeling of luxury in the bath came about from its simplicity," Mike says. Power actually feels that bath is quite understated, but she admits it's an attention getter.

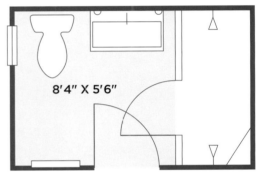

ABOVE: With no room for expansion, the designer removed the old tub and replaced it with a shower.

8'4" X 5'6"

ABOVE: An Italian console sink was the first major fixture chosen for this bathroom. Its look influenced everything else that went into the small space.

TOP RIGHT: Small metallic accents among the larger porcelain floor tiles go a long way in adding luxury.

RIGHT: This frosted-glass wall cabinet fills the role of a medicine cabinet. It's 7 inches deep and framed in ash wood stained to match the vanity.

OPPOSITE: A Buddha figurine minds the expansive, marble-walled shower, which includes a double showerhead and an adjustable hand shower.

MATERIAL WORTH

In Mike Ang's luxurious master bath, the vanity makes the strongest design statement. The deft mix of materials and textures of this piece guided designer Sally Power's choices for the rest of the bath. For the walls, she specified rich Calacata Oro marble tile. Calacata is different from Carrara marble in that it has a creamier field and warmer veining. Quarzo Nero porcelain tiles went on the floor. Porcelain is impervious to bacteria and easier to clean than natural stone, its advocates say. Reflective elements—the glass shower enclosure, mirrored wall, chrome accents and silver paint—and warm wood in the cabinet frame and sink base complete the composition.

Senior Class

HEAVEN IN BATHROOM FORM is what the owners of this 1980s home in Bellevue, Washington, wanted for their master bath. They envisioned what they called "a spa-like retreat," but one with a practical side, too. The design had to accommodate the changing needs of its retired owners as they got older; in other words, it had to allow for aging in place.

Diane Foreman, of The Showplace Design & Remodeling in Redmond, Washington, rose to the occasion with aplomb. The large space meant she'd have plenty of room for features like a steam shower and a bath with body jets. Her challenge, of course, was preserving enough of that large space for someone to make T-turns in a wheelchair.

Foreman used a Japanese concept, combining the shower and bathtub into a "wet room." By keeping the shower open to the bathtub but enclosing both with a custom glass wall, she was able to fit a two-person shower, complete with a rainshower, hand shower, body jets, steam function and bench, plus a two-person air bath, into a fairly compact space.

More rearranging made room for a large vanity top and plenty of storage. The toilet moved from opposite the door to a spot behind a short wall. The original position was unacceptable, because the toilet was the first thing people saw when they walked in.

To create a strong contemporary design statement, another part of her clients' request, Foreman opted for a loose Zen theme, using natural materials inspired by the homeowners' love of the water. For the walls and floor, she chose easy-care ceramic tile in smoky blue tones, graduating the sizes of the tiles to give the effect of a waterfall. The granite vanity top has a variegated pattern that gives the impression of water flowing.

Metallic accents throughout reinforce the contemporary feel. Repeated shape motifs—from the geometric grid of the mosaic tiles to the half-moon of the shower control panel, vessel sink, and granite backsplash—show Foreman's meticulous attention to detail, a quality her clients appreciated.

What they loved even more was that a person with limited mobility could use the bath she crafted. Shortly after the bath was finished, the wife had to have hip-replacement surgery. She called Foreman and proclaimed how beautifully the bath functioned for her after she returned from the hospital. She had to use a walker, and the grab bars and hand shower made things so much easier for her.

PRECEDING PAGES:
Repeating squares, half-
moons and other shapes give
this room aesthetic beauty.
The owners get the most
serenity, however, from the
generous room to maneuver.

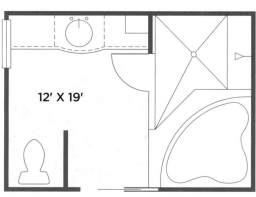

12' X 19'

ABOVE: Beneath the black
headrest on this two-person
tub are a dozen back-
massaging jets; an equal
number of outlets in the tub
floor produce air bubbles.

LEFT: In the end, the
copious floor space all
around increases the worth
of the room exponentially.

RIGHT: Tub and shower exist separately but in a single enclosed space (a wet room), which also boasts steam capabilities.

ABOVE: Metallic elements, not the least of which is this vessel lav, play a key visual role in this contemporary space.

HARD SUBJECTS

To give this master bath the Asian-influenced atmosphere she'd imagined, designer Diane Foreman chose a mix of natural materials. Using ceramic tile throughout—for ease of maintenance and the ability to create stone-like looks—Foreman created patterns of different sizes and shapes to create visual interest and to delineate areas of use within the room. Italian Aran Azul granite makes a no-fuss vanity countertop and adds to the watery effect the designer wanted. Metallic accents lend a contemporary edge, particularly in combination with cabinets of espresso-stained medium-density fiberboard. The overall impression is sleek, yet dynamic—and supremely easy to clean.

RIGHT: Tile treatments are as varied and classy as the shower options. Note the subtle addition of color in the cobalt accents.

Out with Trash, In with Treasure

OPPOSITE: Smoothing out the perimeter of the compact bathroom was key to creating the illusion of spaciousness. Two examples of this strategy in action are the recessed shelves and the low-profile toilet that's partially tucked away into a wall cavity.

BELOW: A wall-mounted faucet clears space on the vanity for toiletries and more.

WHEN ARCHITECT CHARLES SCHWARTZAPFEL bought a two-bedroom apartment in a century-old building in New York City, he immediately made it his own—not by changing the space, but by removing the remnants of its recent history. The horrible wood paneling came off, and the dropped ceilings came out, according to Rachael Judge, a designer with Charles' firm, CRS Designs, Inc., in New York City. Basically, everything that made the place feel small and closed in came out so that Charles, Judge and the rest of the design team could make it brighter, lighter and much more functional. The challenge was getting rid of the junk.

In the apartment's only bathroom, the first step in the renovation process was removing old brown ceramic tile and pulling out 40-year-old plumbing fixtures.

The bathroom dimensions—little more than 5x8 feet—have remained essentially unchanged, and the new fixtures are pretty much where the old ones had been. The difference is that the new versions are more functional, efficient and attractive, and the space no longer feels so dark and claustrophobic. White is the dominant color; it appears on the vanity top, undermount sink, toilet, painted ceiling and upper walls. The lower walls and floor are Portuguese limestone in a pale creamy white with gray undertones; the trim is a rich gray-blue French limestone.

The design team started with 16-inch tiles and had them cut—in half, and in some cases, in half again. The walls comprise 8x16-inch tiles set in a staggered, brick-like pattern. Contrasting 8x16 trim tiles sit just above the floor, and 4x16 gray-blue tiles cap the creamy white limestone and extend around the room. A subtle detail that ties all the elements together is the satin-nickel wainscot edging; it rings the entire room. Charles says the edging was perforated "to allow the stone to read through."

The same two tones of limestone were used on the floor. Within a gray-blue border are 6x6-inch tiles, cut down from the original 16-inch limestone squares and set at a 45-degree angle. The look is almost like carpet, according to Judge.

Overall, the room is spare. The vanity has open shelves for towels, and below those are a pair of 12-inch drawers for bath supplies. Set into the walls are two storage niches. Both openings are

mirror-backed; their reflections add to the volume of light, making the space feel more open and less confined. The niche next to the toilet was once a window that had been boarded up. Charles boxed it in and finished it neatly so that its height is the same as the other niche, even though it is 6 inches narrower.

For unity and simplicity, the same materials repeat throughout the design. Both the shelves and shower door are clear glass; satin-finish nickel graces the fittings and hardware, and the base of the vanity and the frame surrounding the wall mirror are both walnut.

"I wanted to give myself the opportunity, within a very small space, to enjoy the same luxury and simplicity I give my clients," says Charles. "As the design is clean and fluid, the room actually feels bigger than it is."

ABOVE: Mirrors over the sink and behind each shelving niche reflect light and visually expand the space. The vanity contains one open shelf and below it a pair of 12-inch-square drawers for supplies.

RIGHT: Open space above the toilet tank not only allows access for maintenance, it also stretches the room's storage capacity. Pushing the commode into the wall saves floor space.

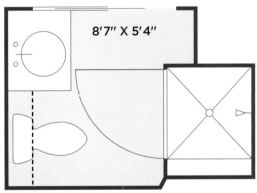

8'7" X 5'4"

ABOVE: Architect Charles Schwartzapfel simplified his bathroom, paring down obtrusive details and integrating storage into the space—all without enlarging the existing footprint.

OPPOSITE: Hinged on the left, a frameless clear-glass door shields the room from water splashing out of the shower. Multiple showerheads, including body sprays and a handheld spout, give the unit spa-like elegance. A thermostat keeps water temperature constant, and three volume controls determine which sprays operate.

What You
Need to Know
About...

Sauna/Steam Showers

ABOVE: Manufacturers' prefab units mean the soothing benefits of getting steamed from the comfort of home have never been easier.

OPPOSITE ABOVE: This pre-built sauna is ready for any available corner of the home. Made of cedar, the unit has a curved-glass door, soft interior lighting and ergonomic seating.

OPPOSITE BELOW: Even the Finns acknowledge that other cultures, including indigenous Americans, have sauna-like traditions. This unit is based on ancient Aztec sweat baths and combines the high heat of a sauna with the vapor action of a steam bath to create a new type of therapeutic shower space.

AFTER A GRUELING DAY at the office, nothing could be better than relaxing in your own personal sauna or steam shower. "The high heat of a sauna or the warm, moist air of a steam bath relaxes muscles, eases tension and drains impurities from the body," says one bath designer, and she should know. The designer in question has had a steam shower in her home for more than 10 years. Of course, she acknowledges that when she installed that steam shower, she was a trendsetter. Such a bathing fixture was considered among the most elite of extravagances to find in a person's home.

Times change, however. According to the National Kitchen & Bath Association, more homeowners are willing to indulge in spa spaces in their homes, places that are equipped with jetted tubs, multispray showers, saunas and steam showers.

IT'S NOT THE HUMIDITY—IT'S THE HEAT

The key distinction between saunas and steam showers is heat vs. humidity. The sauna is all about heat, which should come as little surprise considering it was invented in Finland, a country of 5.1 million people and 1.7 million saunas—one for every three citizens—according to its government. A sauna is a small, wood-lined room that heats up to around 200°F. Traditionally, sauna walls, ceilings, floor slats, doors and benches are built from softwoods such as aspen, redwood or cedar. The reason is that softwoods deflect heat. Hardwoods, like oak, maple, cherry, birch or chestnut, would retain the heat.

The essential component of any sauna is a stove, a wood-burning, gas or electric-powered device, which warms fist-size pieces of granite. The granite stones, in turn, hold and disperse the heat. Of the three types of stoves available, electric models, which run on a standard, 240-volt household electrical connection, are the most common because they are clean and efficient and don't require venting to the outside. Wood and gas designs must have a chimney, and they should also include a carbon monoxide detector to monitor for leaks.

Saunas range in size from petite 4x4-foot boxes to spacious 6 x 10-foot booths. To determine the proper size, consider the available space and the maximum number of users. As a general rule, one manufacturer suggests allowing 65 cubic feet of space for each bather. Using this as a guide, the 4x4-foot unit with a 7-foot ceiling would accommodate only one person, whereas an 8x10-foot space could easily hold nine people. Seven feet is considered the ideal ceiling height for a sauna. It's tall enough for most people, but the warm air won't rise too far out of reach. Conveniently, it also allows saunas to be built inside existing homes.

ROOT, ROOT, ROOT FOR HOME STEAM

If you can't take the heat, get out of the sauna and consider a steam shower instead. Steam showers provide many of the same health benefits as saunas, but they do so in 100 percent humidity rather than a high-heat environment. They typically max out at about 104°F, whereas temperatures in a sauna can approach twice that.

(We'll be using the phrases "steam shower" and "steam bath" interchangeably in this space. In homes, they're pretty much identical.)

Saunas and steam baths differ in space demands, too. Even the smallest saunas require dedicated rooms. Steam baths do not. Their key components (electric generators, thermostats and valves) are sized to fit the dimensions of standard bathtubs or freestanding showers. Add a waterproof ceiling and walls, and an airtight glass door to enclose the space, and that's the basis for a steam bath.

The generator is a relatively small device that converts cold water to hot vapor. It runs off standard 240-volt household electricity. Because of its pint-size proportions, the generator can hide inside any easily accessible cabinet that is no more than 25 feet from the shower.

When selecting a generator, pay close attention to its kilowatt rating—5, 7, 9 and 11 kilowatts are standard. The number of kilowatts indicates the amount of steam the system can produce. A 5-kilowatt generator would work fine for a standard tub/shower application, but it would never produce enough steam to fill a larger 6x10-foot space, according to professional designers. To help find the model that's right for a given steaming area, note the volume of the space (length x width x height) and the type of material that lines the walls, floor and ceiling before heading to the showroom.

Generators come as a package, complete with an outlet and a control pad. The outlet, which should be mounted 6 to 12 inches above the shower floor, dispenses steam into the space, while the pad regulates the time and temperature of the bath. (Tub/shower setups are the exception to the 6-to-12-inch rule; in these setups, the steam head should be mounted 6 inches above the top ledge of the tub.)

MONEY MATTERS

For steam showers, expect to start in the low four digits and go from there, but that's just for the working guts: the generator, output valve and controls. The airtight door and the cosmetics of the wall and ceiling are extra and can go from budget-priced to extravagant. Saunas are usually more expensive than steam spaces, and the bigger the sauna, the higher the price, as about 75 percent of a sauna's cost is wood framing.

GOOD Whether buying a sauna or a steam shower, expect the minimum at this level. With saunas, look for prefabricated units designed to seat no more than three bathers. Wood choices will be limited to the more common softwood species, such as cedar and spruce. For steamers, look for generators sized to accommodate small tub/shower spaces, or portable steam cabinets designed to accommodate individual users. Whether sauna or steam, expect manual time and temperature controls.

BETTER Step up to larger saunas and steam systems, both designed to accommodate two to six people. Where saunas are concerned, look for a wider selection of woods, including such rare species as Alaskan yellow cedar and clear Western hemlock. With steam, look for 7- and 9-kilowatt generators designed to exhale greater quantities of steam, or self-contained capsules that can go anywhere that has access to an electric outlet. Digital controls for both systems begin to appear in this price range, as does an extra set of controls that allow people to turn on the unit before stepping inside.

BEST Size and style are the two reasons to consider these sophisticated saunas and steam showers. With steam, expect to find all the necessary components, but look for them in a partly assembled acrylic frame (similar to a bathtub) that can be dropped into any preplumbed and wired space. Saunas crafted from rare woods and sized to handle eight to 10 people are common. Luxury extras such as recessed interior lighting, music and aromatherapy systems are common for both types of systems.

Toilets

WHAT'S THE WORST THING A TOILET CAN DO? That's right: Fail. Few things are less welcome and potentially embarrassing as toilet failure, and when the first so-called "low-flow" toilets came out, complaints of clogs and double flushing were fairly widespread. Things have changed, thanks to improved engineering and savvy designs.

In 1994, a new Federal law mandated that all new toilets installed in homes could use no more than 1.6 gallons per flush and this was generally regarded as an environmental victory. The old limit was a copious 3.5 gallons, and judging by the performance of the first models, manufacturers appeared taken off guard by the dramatic decrease in flush limits.

THREE WAYS TO 1.6 GALLONS

All of today's toilets work effectively with less water, using one of three basic flushing systems: gravity-fed, pressure-assisted or pump-assisted. Of the three, gravity, which relies on the force of water dropping from the tank into the bowl to remove waste, is the most common. Pressure systems, which use compressed air to force water into and through the bowl, rank a distant second. Possible reasons for the second-place ranking are that these tanks tend to be louder, a little more expensive and more complicated to repair than their gravity-fed counterparts. Pump-assisted designs work much like their pressure-assisted cousins, but with less noise. The downside is they require electricity to operate; if the power's out, so is the toilet.

Those really concerned about water usage might consider a toilet with a dual-flush actuator—a button that allows choosing the number of gallons of water (either 1.6 or 1.1) used with each flush.

DESIGN DECISIONS

Two-piece toilets, bowls attached to separate tanks, are still the most common, but one-piece models, which meld the tank and bowl into a single piece of sculpted china, are gaining ground in the market. One-piece toilets are easier to clean because they avoid the crevices between the bowl and tank. They also usually, but not always, present a lower profile (read: they're shorter), which provides a sleeker, more sophisticated look to a room.

All toilets offer two bowl shapes: round or elongated. Top professional designers say elongated bowls are fast becoming the favorite. They're more comfortable to sit on because the oval shape pro-

BELOW: The architectural lines of this unit illustrate that even the humble commode can contribute a bit of style to the bathroom.

RIGHT: The hidden tank of this imported wall-hung toilet helps to eliminate some cleaning hassles.

BELOW: One-piece toilets have low profiles, which helps small rooms feel larger.

vides better leg support. Elongated bowls are also easier to clean on the inside, because more of the surface area is covered with water. One major disadvantage of elongated bowls, however, is that they stick out an extra 2 inches from the wall—29½ inches, compared to 27½ inches for regular round bowls. This can be a substantial distinction in a small bathroom.

THE RIGHT FIT

Finally, when shopping, consider how the toilet fits the body. Explore so-called "chair height" designs, which are a little higher than usual. Many manufacturers make toilets whose seats rest a full 17 inches off the floor. (The seat height for most toilets is around 15 inches.) The extra 2 inches make it easier to get on and off because there's not as much bending involved. It's a trait that's appreciated by users of all ages and one to consider if planning a universal bathroom.

Prices for toilets start around "anyone-can-afford" and can soar to well past "if-you-have-to-ask-you-can't-afford," depending on style and features. Keep in mind, too, that the price of a toilet—no matter how expensive—does not include the seat. That extra can add anywhere from a couple small bills to a few big ones.

GOOD Look for standard-issue models in white. Round or elongated bowls are available. Two-piece designs are the norm, but one-piece configurations can be had at the upper reaches of this price point.

BETTER Color choices expand to include almond and such relatively eye-catching hues as gray, blue and green. One-piece designs become more common; two-piece models become more decorative. Add-ons include nickel or brass trims for levers and seat hinges. Power-assisted flushing becomes available.

BEST High design is the real reason for choosing a toilet in this price range. Look for one- and two-piece styles that coordinate beautifully with sink and bathtub choices to form what designers call a suite of bathroom products. Dual-flush actuators and heated seats are also common. At this price, it shouldn't just be a toilet; it should be a dimension of design and luxury.

Cabinets

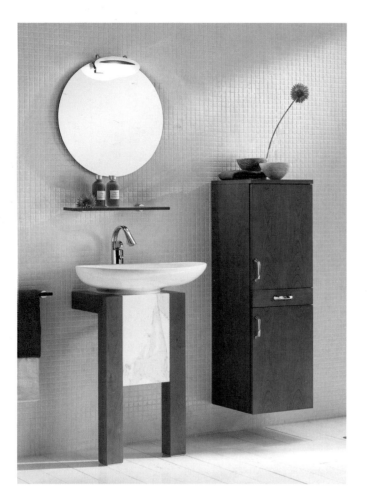

ALTHOUGH BATHROOMS TEND TO BE the smallest rooms in the house, a lot of vital hygiene and pampering activities take place there. As a result, every element needs to contribute, both in terms of function and aesthetics, for a bathroom to be its best. Even cabinets need to perform at a high level. Fortunately, cabinet options abound in every price range.

STOCK

Stock cabinets are the least expensive. These mass-produced units come in standard widths, with depths of 12 inches for upper cabinets and 24 inches for lower ones. They're available at home centers, lumberyards, appliance stores and some showrooms. Particleboard or another composite board, faced with laminate or wood veneer, is the typical building material for stock cabinets. They come pre-assembled and cannot be modified—what you see is what you get. If you don't want fancy finishes, and if your space doesn't require specialized sizing, stock cabinets could be your best bet. This economical option certainly provides storage, and intelligent shopping and design should be able to wring some grace out of stock as well.

RTA (ready to assemble) cabinets will save you even more money. They come packed flat and are made to square up when assembled. The standard tool set needed for the job consists of a screwdriver, tape measure, level and framing square to make certain the cabinets are properly aligned; this will ensure that the doors and drawers operate smoothly. These cabinets require some do-it-yourself savvy and time, but they can be a real bargain if they fit a space's needs.

SEMICUSTOM

Between stock and custom (more on that later) reside semicustom cabinets. They start with a standard set of dimensions and finishes, with modifications available. Height, depth and width measurements are usually fair game, but odd shapes and angles are not available, which is but one area where semicustom falls short of true custom. A limited variety of accessories is also offered.

Because semicustom cabinets are made from higher-grade materials—medium-density fiberboard (MDF) for interiors—and include more options, they cost more than

GOOD Stock. Limited range of basic-quality woods, particleboard or laminates. Limited door styles, hardware and door swing. Pros: Inexpensive, immediately available. Cons: Not as durable, might need assembly. Usually these are cash-and-carry purchases.

BETTER Semicustom. Oak, maple, cherry, melamine. Depending upon the manufacturer, the range of finishes can be surprisingly varied. Pros: Less expensive than custom, but more options than stock. Cons: Not able to modify for unusual space demands; possible delivery delay. Expect six to eight weeks for delivery.

BEST Custom. Solid, high-grade wood selection and construction (including walnut, alder, quarter-sawn oak, teak or mahogany), deluxe hardware. Can accommodate unusual dimensions, angles, detailing; one-of-a-kind finishes, wide range of accessories. Pros: Unique, highest quality. Cons: Expensive. Delivery time is from five weeks up (could be less than semi-custom if cabinetmaker is local; could be much longer).

stock cabinets, but because they start with a few basic components that repeat through lots and lots of cabinets, they're less expensive than custom units.

Surprisingly, delivery time for some semicustom cabinets can actually run longer than for custom cabinets, depending on the cabinetmaker and its location. Semi-custom cabinets might take only three weeks to build, but a large company on the opposite coast from the homeowner or overseas might take another three weeks to fill the truck or container those cabinets are loaded into and ship them to their destination. A small, custom cabinetmaker can deliver cabinets as soon as they're completed.

CUSTOM

Predictably, custom cabinets are the most expensive option. They are made to each customer's exact specifications; the materials, dimensions and style reflect the homeowner's individual preferences and space requirements. These cabinets could be built by a local cabinetmaker, who will make a house call, measure the space and build the cabinets in a workshop. In other cases, a large cabinet company would work with a bathroom designer to create the cabinets.

These cabinets boast the finest hardware and often include such niceties as tilt-out drawers near the sink for hairbrushes and roll-out trays for makeup. The most noticeable difference, however, are in the exterior finishes. In custom cabinets, exotic woods like teak and Wenge are more evident. Glazed, crackled and distressed finishes are available in various colors.

Custom cabinets can resemble fine pieces of furniture. Of course, quality woodwork executed by skilled craftsmen costs a good deal more than stock cabinets. If the budget allows, however, the results will provide a bathroom with rarefied elegance.

OVERALL CONSIDERATIONS

The primary consideration at the heart of any bathroom cabinet is whether it provides adequate storage. Beyond that, the finish—both inside and outside—is there to satisfy the homeowner's personal preferences.

The inside of the drawers and cupboards should be either fully lined with melamine or sealed for easy cleaning. This will also prevent odor absorption of products stored in the unit and, in case of products not made of solid wood (think particleboard, MDF, etc.), the release of gases from materials used in making the cabinets. To extend the life of a wood cabinet, the exterior should have a clear "catalyzed" finish. (This is produced when a chemical catalyzer is added to the varnish, accelerating the dry time and allowing it to harden into a strong finish.)

Beyond these basics, anything goes. New cabinets can be made to resemble vintage pieces, antiques can be modified to accommodate modern plumbing, or state-of-the-art fixtures can be paired with the latest in cabinet materials and design.

No matter what your budget, you can furnish your bathroom with cabinets that have purpose as well as pizzazz.

ABOVE: Custom cabinets, like those shown, are tailor-made down to the last inch.

OPPOSITE: A wall-mounted cabinet offers open access to the floor and is therefore a natural in contemporary design motifs.

LEFT: Large drawer bins provide diverse storage opportunities—for bath linens, paper goods or cleaning supplies.

Jetted Tubs

MANY VACATIONERS REJOICE IN THE REJUVENATION they get from a jetted tub. Often, it's their first experience with such a tub, and more and more people are wanting to replicate that experience at home. That may be why the Department of Commerce says the percentage of U.S. homes with a jetted tub has hit double digits.

BUBBLE YOUR PLEASURE

For those contemplating the cornerstone spa amenity, the first thing to learn is that jetted tubs actually come in two types: whirlpool tubs and air baths. Whirlpool tubs were invented by Roy Jacuzzi. (Yes, he's a real person, and he's quite wealthy.) The "whirl" comes from the jets that mix air and water to create massaging bubbles. In general, a higher proportion of air to water means a stronger massage. More water than air translates to a gentler stream. Air baths create fizzy, all-around bubbles instead of a more targeted and pulsating effect. This is because the air outlets that move the water are tiny (about the size of a pin head) and encircle the bottom of the tub.

MATERIAL ISSUES

Like ordinary baths, jetted tubs are made from one of three materials: enameled cast iron, acrylic or fiberglass. Of the three, cast iron is the most durable and the heaviest, and consequently, the most expensive. It is also the most rigid, which limits the range of shapes and sizes.

Acrylic is not only lighter, it's also a good choice for unusual shapes. Acrylic can be molded into almost any configuration, and it resists stains, chipping and cracking. Because the color runs all the way through, nicks and scratches can be buffed out. Like acrylic models, fiberglass tubs are light and come in a variety of shapes and sizes. The downside is that because fiberglass is an inherently "soft" material, the surface scratches and stains more easily than acrylic.

Another consideration in selecting a tub is the capacity of the home's water heater. Larger tubs can hold in excess of 100 gallons. Those whose water heaters can't handle the load will either have to choose smaller tubs, select tubs with built-in heaters, or upgrade their homes' water heaters. Larger tubs (especially those made of cast iron) can also become extremely heavy when filled with water and may require beefed-up structural framing for support.

SIZES AND SHAPES

Size and shape depends primarily on available space. Ovals, rectangles, ellipses and radius-ended silhouettes are the most traditional shapes, although with moldable acrylic and fiberglass, corner tubs and other unusual configurations are possible. Common dimensions include: 5½ feet x 32 inches (standard), 5½ feet x 34 inches, 6 feet x 36 inches, and for double occupancy, 6½ feet x 39 inches.

BELOW: Complete customization is the name of the game with this whirlpool bath. Consumers have a choice of 20 distinct water-treatment options that range from calming effervescent bubbles to revitalizing brisk hydromassage. A lighted control keypad allows the user to easily adjust the flow and temperature of the water. The tub also includes a handy remote control that floats.

OPPOSITE ABOVE: This bath offers a transitional freestanding design that blends old-world charm with contemporary styling. A double-wall design of reinforced acrylic conceals the strategically placed air jets in the bottom of the bath. The jets are controlled with an electronic keypad and flow rate ranges from gentle to vigorous.

Consider the depth of the bathing well, too—the distance from the bottom of the tub to the emergency overflow drain. For optimum comfort, it should be a minimum of 20 inches. Anything shallower could deprive bathers of the full benefit of the jets because they won't be under the water.

Buying decisions shouldn't be based solely on size, however. Most whirlpools and air-jet baths have ergonomically designed interiors to support the body's curves. When shopping, ask if it's OK to hop in a tub. It won't feel the same as when it's full of water, but it will provide an idea of how comfortable the tub is. Footrests and headrests affect the fit of these baths, especially if the user is particularly tall or petite.

OPERATING SYSTEMS

Because a whirlpool or air-jet tub is about relaxing, it is important to consider the mechanism that moves the water around the tub. If the jets are in the wrong place, the tub won't be as comfortable to use.

When shopping for a whirlpool, look for a tub with fully adjustable jets positioned at key pressure points (head, shoulders, back, hips and feet). Also, look for a model with multiple power levels so you can increase or decrease the pulsating pressure of the moving water.

For an air bath, look for a tub with air channels that circle the entire perimeter. Some value-priced models put jet openings near key pressure points only, but to make full use of the tub, the openings should cover every part of the body, experts say. Also, look for at least a 600-watt blower. Otherwise the warm air may not make it to the feet.

Although quieter, tubs aren't silent. Shop for a well-insulated tub with a suspended motor and pump assembly. Consider having the motor installed in a remote but accessible location, such as an adjacent closet.

For a truly luxurious bathing experience, consider adding some deluxe features, such as chromatherapy, which is an add-on option that washes the bather in a pool of light, or a built-in music system.

CARE AND MAINTENANCE

Unlike standard tubs, whirlpools and air baths require regular maintenance beyond wiping down the acrylic or porcelain basin. To be sure, follow the manufacturer's instructions, but generally a whirlpool tub's jets should be flushed at least once a month with a cleaning solution to remove dirt from inside the jets. Special spa cleaners are available, and many tub makers offer their own brands, but a solution of water and a *low-foaming* dishwasher detergent will do the job. To clean an air bath, simply press a button that sends air through the system to purge the channels of standing water. This should be done each time the tub is used.

In both cases, avoid using bath oils or other similar products in the tub. They may clog jets and can damage some surfaces.

GOOD These tubs are available in sizes that can accommodate one or two bathers. Basic shapes, simple styling and four to six jets are common. On/off air switches are also standard. In-line heaters, which help maintain a consistent water temperature, and timers that stop the water from moving after the first 20 minutes cost extra.

BETTER Look for single- and double-size tubs with a little more design pizzazz and a few more features. In-line heaters, deeper bathing wells, and additional jets are popular extras. Electronic controls allow you to regulate jets individually.

BEST At a minimum, these high-style tubs feature six to eight fully adjustable jets, and most accommodate at least two bathers. "Better" extras, such as electronic controls and in-line heaters, are standard. Such amenities as a mood-lighting system can be found at the upper end of this price category.

ULTRA For the ultimate in spa-style luxury, look for models with anywhere from eight to 10 adjustable, electronically controlled jets designed to massage the body from head to toe. Also, expect a host of relaxing extras, such as underwater lighting systems, flat-screen televisions, DVD players and stereo systems—and don't forget the remote.

Surfaces

WE DEMAND SO MUCH of bathroom surfaces: They need to be impervious to high traffic, resistant to mildew-causing moisture and sturdy enough to withstand industrial-strength cleaning. Through all this, they need to look good, too. Nobody wants a bathroom that looks like a high school locker room. Many, however, would be quite pleased with a room made of no-fuss materials designed to resemble a luxury spa, or at least a classy hotel room they once stayed in. Fortunately, practical good looks are available at every price point in all three main bathroom surfaces: walls, countertops and flooring.

WALLS

Durability and safety should be primary concerns when choosing bathroom surface materials. Durability is especially key in the wall department. In order to stand up to the constant deluge of water, walls in the "wet" areas of a bathroom—the sink, tub and shower sections—demand the sturdiest materials. Tiles, glass or acrylic block and natural stone are waterproof, easy to clean and, yes, durable. Then again, nobody ever said, "I want that durable, hideous wall material there." So thank the stars that these materials also present a wealth of aesthetic options.

Ceramic tiles are sold individually or in sheets of small mosaics. They come in a panorama of colors, shapes and sizes. The bread and butter of bathroom tile is a 4¼-inch square white tile, It's likely to be among the most inexpensive wall surfaces available, which is great for those who want a lot of standard white tile in their bathrooms. On the flip side, imported glazed porcelain mosaics and other fancy hand-made tiles qualify as expensive materials based on square foot price, and none of this takes into account installation cost.

Glass or acrylic block can function as a wall or room divider while adding ambient light without sacrificing privacy. On the whole, glass is more expensive than acrylic, and acrylic block is considered a moderate-priced surface option.

Stone tiles add a welcome natural element to the bathroom for a price equivalent to expensive ceramic tile. In wall applications, these tiles must be sealed in order to prevent staining or erosion from cleaning products.

For the "dry" areas of the bathroom—places where water won't be splashed onto the surface and where steam won't leak out—seek out paint and wallpaper that are specifically manufactured for bathroom use. Gloss or semigloss paint has a high resin content, which means it should hold up. Seek out paints with mildew-resistant additives—or you can ask your paint dealer to add a fungicide to standard paint. The fungicide could add about 10 percent to the price of a quality paint. For wallcoverings, the best bet is solid vinyl wallpaper. Prices vary to the point where the same room could cost three times as much, depending on wallpaper choice.

COUNTERTOPS

Look for countertop materials that can be splashed on and wiped down when you clean. The ceramic tile that performs beautifully on the wall will do the same on your counters. Laminate, cultured marble, solid surfacing, quartz surfacing and stone are also durable, water-resistant options. Wood isn't the best choice as it tends to discolor, warp or decay when exposed to water. (Specialty companies make fixtures made of resin-impregnated wood that will stand up to water. This is different from most interior-grade wood, which is not water's friend.)

Laminate comes in many colors, textures and patterns and is the least expensive countertop material. Unfortunately, it can scratch, chip and stain and is difficult to repair. Cultured marble is a cast polymer—a mixture of a resin and crushed stone that has been molded. It tends to be less expensive and is easy to clean but is prone to cracks.

Solid-surfacing materials are nonporous, heat resistant, water resistant, repairable and easy to clean. However, they come in a smaller range of colors and are significantly more expensive than either laminate or cultured marble.

Unlike natural stone, quartz-based surfaces are nonporous and stain and scratch resistant, making them a smart selection for vanity tops. Quartz surfaces are comparable in price to slab stone; both materials lend an elegant, natural appearance to the bathroom.

OPPOSITE, TOP TO BOTTOM: Wood laminate surfacing, antique stone, laminate countertops, ceramic tile, quartz surfacing

MATERIAL	COST	PROS	CONS	MAINTENANCE
CULTURED MARBLE	Inexpensive	Easy to clean; often has an integral sink	Not that durable; hard to repair	Wash with mild detergent as needed; rinse thoroughly, wipe dry
PLASTIC LAMINATE	Inexpensive	Wide range of colors, textures, patterns; can install yourself	May scratch, chip or stain; layers may separate; hard to repair	Wash with mild liquid or powdered detergents as needed; rinse thoroughly, wipe dry
PAINT	Typically inexpensive; add extra for fungicide	Easy to apply; many colors	Will need a backsplash around sink; can't be used in shower	Vacuum first to remove loose material; wash with mild detergent and water
VINYL WALLPAPER	Moderate	Many options	May hide fungal growth; may peel or bubble	Dust or vacuum frequently; wash with a mild detergent and water as necessary; never use abrasive cleansers
ACRYLIC BLOCK	Moderate	Lightweight; waterproof; allows for ambient light; warmer to touch than glass block	Can scratch; limited sizes	Wash with a mild soap and water or with products approved for plastics; avoid gritty cleaning products and brushes
GLASS BLOCK	Expensive	Durable; waterproof; allows for ambient light	Expensive; needs professional installation	Wash with a mild detergent as needed, rinse and wipe dry
QUARTZ SURFACING	Expensive	Durable; water, heat, stain and scratch resistant; easy to clean	Expensive; best with professional installation	Wash with warm soapy water or mild household cleaners; no sealing needed
SOLID SURFACING	Expensive	Durable; water and heat resistant; easy to clean; can be installed with an integral sink	Expensive; must be installed by a professional; limited color selection	Wash with a mild detergent or powdered cleanser as needed; rinse thoroughly and wipe dry
STONE TILES	Expensive	Durable; easy to clean and maintain; elegant appearance	Expensive; requires professional installation; cold to the touch	Dust or vacuum weekly; wash with a mild detergent as necessary; avoid alkaline cleaners
CERAMIC TILES	Variable—ranges from quite inexpensive to luxurious imports	Durable; easy to clean; can achieve a wide variety of looks	Solid substrate essential to avoid cracking; grout may attract mildew	Clean spills promptly to avoid staining grout; wash with a mild detergent as needed or clean thoroughly with a nonabrasive cleanser

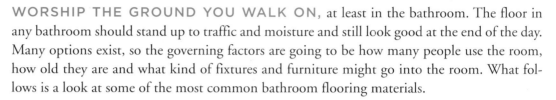

Floors

WORSHIP THE GROUND YOU WALK ON, at least in the bathroom. The floor in any bathroom should stand up to traffic and moisture and still look good at the end of the day. Many options exist, so the governing factors are going to be how many people use the room, how old they are and what kind of fixtures and furniture might go into the room. What follows is a look at some of the most common bathroom flooring materials.

VINYL

Vinyl falls under the umbrella of resilient flooring. (This category also includes linoleum, rubber and cork.) The least expensive in this family, vinyl is also one of the easiest materials to install. Made of solid vinyl or polyurethane, it is a flexible, durable and easy-to-maintain surface. Vinyl also comes in a panoply of colors, textures and patterns.

Because it comes in sheets up to 12 feet wide, vinyl flooring can often be installed without seaming together several pieces. Tiles—generally 12 inches square—are another option, but correct installation is essential to avoid moisture gathering between the tiles.

CERAMIC AND PORCELAIN

Ceramic tile is made from hard-fired slabs of clay. It is extremely durable, moisture-resistant and easy to maintain, and common flooring sizes include 12-inch, 13-inch and 18-inch squares. Sealed grout has eliminated many past bugaboos (mildew, darkening, etc). Tile comes in hundreds of patterns, colors, shapes and finishes, and it is legendarily versatile. Mixing tiles of different sizes, shapes and colors is not only permissible, it's the height of fashion.

Ceramic tiles can be unglazed or glazed. Porcelain pavers are made of a different type of clay than standard ceramic tile and fired at a higher temperature. They are more dense, and thus more durable than ceramic tiles.

LAMINATE

Laminate flooring is made of layers of paper impregnated with resins and compressed into a wear-resistant composite on top of a synthetic backing. It comes in planks or tiles that look like wood, stone or ceramic tile. Some varieties, however, eschew look-alikes in favor of their own distinctive appearance. In general, laminate flooring is more durable than one might imagine, and with a soft underlayment, it's easy on the legs.

Laminate flooring is not difficult to install, particularly if it's a glueless product that clicks into place. Because it's a floating floor, meaning the pieces are attached to each other, not the foam subflooring, it can be a little noisy. Acoustical padding can counteract the echo effect.

SOLID WOOD

Laminate floors can duplicate the look of wood, but they can't quite capture its character. The moisture issue makes wood better suited to kitchens than baths, but a few natural wood accents can make a dramatic impact. For example, alternate strips of light and dark stained woods can create a contemporary, graphic statement. Be aware, however, that they may wear unevenly and be difficult to repair. A wise, judicious approach to wood is best in the bathroom.

ENGINEERED HARDWOOD

Made of hardwood layers glued together so that the grains run in different directions, an engineered plank is more dimensionally stable and moisture resistant than solid wood. A possible disadvantage of engineered hardwood is is that it cannot be refinished as many times as solid hardwood. Engineered hardwood advocates counter that solid wood floors can only be refinished down to the nail head, which sits ¼ inch below the surface of the wood—the same depth of the top layer of an engineered floor.

CARPET

Wall-to-wall carpeting in a room with lots of water and humidity is like wearing wet socks (and shoes) 24 hours a day—just flat-out unhealthy. A modular carpet system, however, allows damp tiles to be removed, dried and replaced. Shop around, though: some systems are easier to work with than others.

LEFT: Carpet in the bath is usually silly, but these modular tiles are stylish and easy to replace when doused or if damaged.

OPPOSITE, TOP AND MIDDLE: Moisture-resistant ceramic tiles are a good bet for the bath and other wet areas of the home.
BOTTOM: Resilient vinyl flooring, like these tiles, comes in a broad array of colors and textures for endless design possibilities.

MATERIAL	COST	PROS	CONS	LIFE SPAN	MAINTENANCE	DURABILITY
VINYL	Inexpensive	Moisture and stain resistant; flexible; available in a wide variety of designs	Requires significant floor prep work; vulnerable to dents and tears	10 to 15 years	Easy. Damp mop with a product made for vinyl to avoid streaking	Medium
LAMINATE	Inexpensive to Moderate	Easy to maintain; easy to install; can resemble wood or stone	Doesn't have the "depth" of wood or stone; noisy; can't be refinished	10 to 20 years	Easy. Don't over-wet the floor when mopping	High
PORCELAIN PAVERS	Moderate	Extremely durable form of tile; stone-like look; rougher surfaces good for bath	Cold; noisy; difficult to stand on for long periods; requires some skill to install	Lifetime	Low. Sweep and damp mop as needed	Very high
CERAMIC TILE	Variable	Durable; easy to maintain; versatile	Cold; noisy; slippery; difficult to stand on for long periods	Lifetime	Low. Sweep and damp mop as needed	Very high
SOLID WOOD	Moderate to Expensive	Natural look; warm; can be refinished	Can suffer moisture damage	Lifetime	Moderate. Refinish every 6 to 8 years. Sweep, vacuum and lightly damp mop as needed	Very high
ENGINEERED HARDWOOD	Moderate to Expensive	More moisture resistant than solid wood	Not impervious to water or staining; limited refinishing options	Lifetime	Moderate. Refinish every 6 to 8 years. sweep, vacuum with a brush and lightly damp mop	Very high

Windows

BATHROOM WINDOWS CAN MAKE AN IMPACT not only on the view from the inside but also on how a home looks from the outside. After all, neighbors may never see the new whirlpool tub, but they'll notice a home's windows on a daily basis. Furthermore, windows can be one of the biggest-ticket items in a budget. With that in mind, homeowners should strive for no less than the best built, most energy-efficient windows they can buy.

Windows and doors have more impact on the outside and the inside of a home than any other building product, yet many people spend more time choosing paint colors and countertop materials. Windows convey personality to the outside world as well as framing the view from inside the home. Plus, choosing the right windows can reduce the time and effort spent maintaining the exterior of the home. So careful, thorough research is essential to ensure maximum bang for the investment.

Whether replacing an existing window or specifying windows for new construction, factors to consider include framing material, the glass and style of the window.

WINDOW FRAMES

Window frames are made of a number of different materials such as wood, vinyl, and wood wrapped in aluminum or plastic. The least expensive option is the vinyl frame, primarily the province of replacement windows. For example, a 3x3-foot vinyl-framed window would be about half the price as the same-size window with a primed-wood frame. On a big project, that can add up to considerable savings.

Those trying to match existing windows in an older home may have no choice but to turn to wood. The versatility of wood allows it to take on any desired color. On top of that, its classic appearance lends value to any home. Wood frames can have a long life span, but on the downside, they're more susceptible to the elements than metal or vinyl. Accordingly, wood frames typically entail ongoing costs for repainting or refinishing.

Window frames that are wood on the inside of the home but have a protective coating outside combine wood's insulation with the durability of man-made materials. This cladding, as it's called, is usually aluminum and can be thin (roll-form) or thick (extruded), based on how it is produced. Roll-form aluminum is as thick as a soda can, whereas extruded aluminum is about as thick as a quarter. In either form, aluminum won't fade, chalk, chip or crack as easily as paint.

Some companies use a combination of both techniques to suit the different functions of each frame component. For example, some aluminum-clad windows are made with roll-form sashes and extruded frames.

GOOD Expect a solid, functional window with a hollow, vinyl frame. Only standard sizes and colors are available at the starter prices. Double glazings are standard, but with plain old air gaps only.

BETTER That hollow vinyl is now solid vinyl. Windows with wood on the interior and a cladding, typically aluminum, on the home's exterior are now within reach. Energy-efficient technologies start to come into play as well, like low-e glass and argon or krypton gas that is pumped between the glazings before they are sealed. Among the energy-efficient windows, however, options are limited at this price point.

BEST Look for more options on clad windows, including a choice of cladding colors and custom wood species. Specialized hardware can also be found at the top of the line, including oil-rubbed bronze finishes. Those on a budget can also get glass in patterns such as obscured, pebbles or cascade. Controlled-view glazings are another possibility. Custom sizes and shapes are available as well.

This allows a higher percentage of wood in the window frame, which makes for better insulation properties.

Although clad-frame windows may appear to be painted wood from a distance, up close the simulation is far less convincing. Another disadvantage is that aluminum-clad windows generally come in a limited range of popular colors—white, off-white and brown may be as far as it goes at many outlets. Custom hues are available, but expect to pay a price; they can cost up to one-third more than all-wood windows.

GLAZING

For the uninitiated, glazing is the window industry's word for a sheet of glass, what many might think of as a pane. Double-glazing, insulated windows have become standard issue these days. Unlike the single-pane windows of the past, insulated windows take the two glazings and trap a layer of gas between them. Sometimes that gas is just air, but some manufacturers fill that pocket up with argon—a colorless, odorless, nontoxic gas with 30 percent less thermal conductivity than air. This reduces the transfer of heat from the inside to the outside and vice versa.

To reduce energy transfer through the glass itself, many windows also come with a low-emissivity (low-e) coating. The difference in appearance is negligible; from the exterior, there's a slightly gray cast in bright sunlight and a slightly green tint at night. But the coating is definitely worth the energy savings. Test homes found a 30 percent reduction in the average afternoon demand for air conditioning when using low-e glass.

STYLE

Most major window manufacturers offer an extensive collection of operable windows—double-hung, casement, awning, hoppers and sliders, for example. They'll also build custom windows to fit the particular demands of any home's bathroom.

Figuring out the overall dimensions of windows is only part of the plan. After that comes settling on the configuration, and the options abound. A window could be one full expanse of glass, or it can be divided into true individual panes, or lights. It can be a little of both, too, with removable snap-on grilles or permanent exterior and interior grilles known as "simulated divided lights" (SDL) applied to full windows. The price of basic windows can rise about 10 percent with a simple clip-on mullion divider or nearly 50 percent with an SDL system.

ENERGY

The National Fenestration Rating Council (NFRC), a non-profit organization based in Silver Spring, Maryland, provides consumers with information that allows them to compare and evaluate energy performance of windows, doors and skylights. To that end, the NFRC has developed a label that rates several of these important properties. These labels appear on most new and replacement windows on the market today. The information these labels contain should help consumers decide which windows are best for their homes.

OPPOSITE ABOVE: A large, multi-paned window brings in gobs of light.

OPPOSITE BELOW: This sliding window is obscured for privacy.

TOP: Strategic design ushers in sun yet still protects bathers' privacy.

ABOVE: The only window in this bath is nevertheless a welcome source of natural light.

CONTACT THE DESIGNERS

National Kitchen & Bath Association
687 Willow Grove Street
Hackettstown, NJ 07840
Phone: (800) 843-6522
www.nkba.com

PAGES 8–9 & 11
Steven M. Levine, CKD, CBD,
and Susan B. Brisk, CKD
Euro-Plus Design
27 Sedgemeadow Road
Wayland, MS 01778
Phone: (508) 358-5392
146 Genesee Lane
Madison, CT 06443
Phone: (203) 421-9326
www.euro-plus.com

PAGE 14
Rhonda Knoche, CKD
Neil Kelly Designers Remodelers
804 N. Alberta Street
Portland, OR 97217
Phone: (503) 288-7461
www.neilkelly.com

PAGES 18–19
Dianna Holmes, CKD
Canac
360 John Street
Thornhill, ON L3T 3M9
Canada
Phone: (905) 881-2153
www.canackitchens.com

PAGES 20–23
Dana Jones, CKD
The Kitchen Consultant
Long Beach, CA 90815
Phone: (562) 431-1911
www.kitchenadvice.com

PAGES 24–27
Erica Westeroth, CKD, and Tim Scott
XTC Design Inc.
39 Marina Avenue
Toronto, ON M8W 1K4
Canada
Phone: (416) 491-9444
www.xtcdesign.com

PAGES 30–35
Jeannie Fulton
Ulrich Inc.
100 Chestnut Street
Ridgewood, NJ 07450
Phone: (201) 445-1260
www.ulrichkitchens.com

PAGES 36–40
Diane Bohstedt, CKD
Insignia Kitchen & Bath Design Group
1435 South Barrington Road
Barrington, IL 60010
Phone: (847) 381-7950
www.insigniakitchenandbath.com

PAGES 44–49
Dianna Holmes, CKD
Canac
360 John Street
Thornhill, ON L3T 3M9
Canada
Phone: (905) 881-2153
www.canackitchens.com

PAGES 50–53
Jason Simonetty
Lee Kimball Kitchens
70 Canal Street
Boston, MA 02114
Phone: (617) 227-0250
www.leekimball.com

PAGES 54–57
Cynthia McClure, CKD
Art Design Build
4309 Lynbrook Drive
Bethesda, MD 20814
Phone: (301) 656-6500
www.artdesignbuild.com

PAGES 60–61
Susan Waters
Insignia Kitchen & Bath Design Group
1435 South Barrington Road
Barrington, IL 60010
Phone: (847) 381-7950
www.insigniakitchenandbath.com

PAGES 62–65
Susan Waters
Insignia Kitchen & Bath Design Group
1435 South Barrington Road
Barrington, IL 60010
Phone: (847) 381-7950
www.insigniakitchenandbath.com

PAGES 66–69
Tess Giuliani, CKD
Tess Giuliani Designs
635 Spring Avenue
Ridgewood, NJ 07450
Phone: (201) 445-7302

PAGES 72–75
Connie Schey
Insignia Kitchen & Bath Design Group
1435 South Barrington Road
Barrington, IL 60010
Phone: (847) 381-7950
www.insigniakitchenandbath.com

PAGES 78–80
Cynthia McClure, CKD
Art Design Build
4309 Lynbrook Drive
Bethesda, MD 20814
Phone: (301) 656-6500
www.artdesignbuild.com

PAGES 84–87
Erica Westeroth, CKD
XTC Design Inc.
39 Marina Avenue
Toronto, ON M8W 1K4
Canada
Phone: (416) 491-9444
www.xtcdesign.com

PAGES 88–89
Erica Westeroth, CKD
XTC Design Inc.
39 Marina Avenue
Toronto, ON M8W 1K4
Canada
Phone: (416) 491-9444
www.xtcdesign.com

PAGES 90–95
David Raber, CKD
Classic Kitchens of Virginia
401 North Ridge Road
Richmond, VA 23229
Phone: (804) 285-2858
www.classickitchensofva.com

PAGES 100–103
Beverly Staal, CKD
The Showplace Design & Remodeling
8710 Willows Road NE
Redmond, WA 98052
Phone: (425) 885-1595
www.showplaceinc.com

PAGE 104–107
Erica Westeroth, CKD
XTC Design Inc.
39 Marina Avenue
Toronto, ON M8W 1K4
Canada
Phone: (416) 491-9444
www.xtcdesign.com

PAGES 110–113
Heather Moe
South Pacific Kitchen
& Construction, Inc.
1541 Santa Margarita Drive
Fallbrook, CA 92028
Phone: (858) 459-9086
www.southpacifickitchenandcon.com

PAGES 114–117
Sally Power
Sally Power Interiors
Sobel Design Building
680 Eighth Street, Suite 204
San Francisco, CA 94103
Phone: (415) 621-9991
www.powerinteriors.com

PAGES 118–121
Diane Foreman, CKD
The Showplace Design & Remodeling
8710 Willows Road NE
Redmond, WA 98052
Phone: (425) 885-1595
www.showplaceinc.com

PAGES 122–125
Charles R. Schwartzapfel, AIA
CRS Designs, Inc.
45 West 45th Street
New York, NY 10036
Phone: (212) 869-1666
www.crsdesigns.com

CREDITS

Thanks to all the designers, photographers, stylists and writers whose work appears in this book.

Design Talk pp. 8–9, Steven M. Levine and Susan B. Brisk; p. 14; Rhonda Knoche, designers.

Authors of original stories: pp. 20–23, 24–27, 36–40, 44–49, 66–69, 84–87, 110–113, 122–125, Mervyn Kaufman; pp. 30–35, Rebecca Winzenried; pp. 50–53; 62–65, 90–95, 100–103, Patricia Connell; pp. 54–57, Theresa McTammany; pp. 72–75, John Loecke; pp. 78–80, 104–107, Kristina Sigler; pp. 114–117, 118–121, Amanda Lecky

Photographs: pp. 8–9, 50–53, Eric Roth; p. 14, David Papazian; pp. 18–19, 44–49, John Gould Bessler; pp. 20–23, Mark Lohman; pp. 24–27, 84–87, 88–89, 104–107, Robin Stubbert; pp. 30–35, 66–69, Melabee M. Miller; pp. 36–40, 54–57, 60–61; 62–65, 72–75, 78–80, Gridley & Graves; pp. 90–95, Steve Budman; pp. 100–103, 118–121, Alex Hayden; pp. 110–113, Edward Gohlich; pp. 114–117, davidduncanlivingston.com; pp. 122–125, Ryan Benyi; all other photos are from manufacturers.